# THE
# *Relationship*
# UPGRADE

PROVEN STRATEGIES FOR A HEALTHIER, HAPPIER AND STRONGER PARTNERSHIP IN THE MODERN DIGITAL WORLD

**ADITI JASRA**
MACP, MBA, RCC, CCC
WELLNESS NORTH COUNSELLING

One Printers Way
Altona, MB R0G 0B0
Canada

www.friesenpress.com



ISBN
978-1-03-919090-0 (Hardcover)
978-1-03-919089-4 (Paperback)
978-1-03-919091-7 (eBook)

1. FAMILY & RELATIONSHIPS, MARRIAGE

Distributed to the trade by The Ingram Book Company

# Contents

# Acknowledgements

I have so many people to express gratitude towards who've helped me bring this idea to life. I am deeply grateful to my husband, Manoj, for his unwavering support and encouragement throughout the process of writing this book as well as for continuously allowing me to assess the quality of our own relationship and those of the people in our lives. His constant belief in me and his willingness to listen to my ideas and provide valuable feedback from a non-clinician standpoint have been invaluable.

I would also like to express my heartfelt gratitude to my own mentors, therapists, and coaches, for their guidance and support throughout my journey and career. Their wisdom and experience have been invaluable in helping me to develop as a counsellor, clinician, and writer, and to be a source of light and guidance for others.

I am also grateful to my clients—who trust me to help them navigate complex relationship journeys—and to my colleagues, for providing me with the opportunity to work on interesting and challenging cases and for their support and collaboration.

I am thankful to my children, for being patient with me as I continued to work on this project as opposed to spending quality time with them, and to my mother for her love and encouragement. Without their support, this project would not have seen the light of the day.

Finally, I would like to thank my readers for their interest in my work and for taking the time to read this book. I hope it will be as enjoyable and informative for you to read as it was for me to write.

# From the Author

As a trained therapist and someone with more than four decades of lived relationship experience, interacting with people from diverse backgrounds and cultures, I have always been fascinated by relationships and how people in partnerships interacted with each other.

My intention through this book is to share useful, objective, and accurate information devoid of as much personal bias as possible. My insights and recommendations are practical, evidence-based, clinically sound, and include my experience studying a wide variety of sources—including academic books and peer-reviewed journals, along with discussions with colleagues, supervisors and mentors, and a wide variety of clientele. I have trained with a number of modern therapeutic methods, including Emotionally Focused Therapy and the Gottman method. I have a wide knowledge base and experience applying it.

I hope that if you feel stuck in your relationship, this book can help you reset and renew the quality of your bond with your partner.

To share your feedback, please drop me a line at ajasra@wellnessnorth.ca or visit my clinic's website at www.wellnessnorth.ca

**Disclaimer**: Please note that all names have been changed to protect the identity of the clients, and some conversations have been paraphrased to allow me to share the gist of the conversation without airing my clients' private matters.

Although I am a therapist, I am probably not *your* therapist. Reading this book does not create a client-counsellor relationship between us. This guide should not be used as a substitute for the advice of a competent and a trained counsellor authorized to practice in your jurisdiction.

I don't make any guarantees about the results of the information shared in this book. I share educational and informative research that is intended to help you upgrade your relationships through simple, pragmatic tips. However, your ultimate success or failure in your relationships will be the result of your own efforts, your particular situation, and innumerable other circumstances beyond my knowledge and control.

# Introduction

## Why should you pick up this book?

Are you ready to upgrade the quality of your relationship?

Whether you're single and ready to mingle, happily taken, in a complicated relationship, or navigating a challenging marriage, this book is for you. It is designed to provide you with clear insights, simple but useful tools, and practical strategies for creating and maintaining healthy, fulfilling connections with your significant others or your better halves.

In these pages, you'll find digestible, research-based advice on some important topics, including communication, resolving differences, building trust, and maintaining intimacy. We'll explore common challenges that arise in adult romantic relationships and offer practical guidance on how to overcome them. Whether you're seeking to strengthen an existing bond or searching for ways to improve your communication and connection with others, this book will be a valuable guide.

### You'll enjoy this read if
- you want to gain a better understanding of your relationships and what makes them work,
- you want to learn about the positive and negative effects technology can have on relationships, or
- you're looking for a survey of important factors that can help you build and maintain healthy partnerships.

So, grab your favourite drink and a cozy blanket, or lounge by the pool lathered up in sunscreen, and get ready to dive into the world of modern-day adult romantic relationships. We hope you find these pages both informative and inspiring as you work to build and maintain meaningful connections with your loved ones.

# CHAPTER 1

———

# #Mutuals

## Healthy partnerships in the digital age

There is absolutely no denying the fact that when it comes to our overall health, well-being, and happiness, the quality of our relationships plays a major role. Human beings are social animals, and our survival depends on our bonds with others. In infancy, we depend on adults in our lives, and in adulthood, a lot of this emotional dependence shifts to our partners.

Strong, healthy, and balanced adult romantic relationships can provide us with love, support, and a sense of belonging. Unhealthy or toxic relationships can have the opposite effect and make our lives miserable. Although it's not the case for everyone, many of us can feel an emptiness in our lives in the absence of a supportive significant other. In my therapeutic work, I've seen the impact of healthy and unhealthy relationships on a person's well-being and mental state numerous times. Our social engagement and connections strongly dictate the quality of our lives.

Of course, relationships take a different level of priority in everyone's lives: we each get to determine how important our relationships are to us. We decide whether our romantic relationships matter more to us than other hats we wear every day—like professional growth, academic success, caretaking, or personal health.

Let's further explore why healthy relationships are so important and look at the benefits they offer.

### *The Benefits of Healthy Relationships*

Since the beginning of the COVID-19 pandemic, many of us have had a huge perspective shift regarding what is truly important for us and what we need to live a fulfilling and meaningful life. Deep down, in some way, shape, or form, we all know that our positive relationships can provide us with unparalleled love, support, and a strong sense of belonging. They have the power and pull to enrich our lives and make the world a worthy place to live.

First and foremost, healthy relationships are essential for our emotional well-being. When we have supportive, loving relationships, we feel more confident, secure, and positive about ourselves. Yes, you read that right—a healthy relationship can influence your self-esteem and confidence. We're more likely to feel good about ourselves and our lives when we have supportive people around us. Frankly speaking, all the evidence points out that we're less likely to suffer from anxiety, depression, or other mental health issues if we are surrounded by loving, compassionate, supportive human beings.

**A big piece of the puzzle here is the concepts of co-regulation and mirror neurons.** Co-regulation is a concept that describes how people in relationships can influence and regulate each other's emotions and behaviours. It's a process through which individuals in any close relationship (such as friends, family, or romantic partners) help each other manage their emotions, thoughts, and actions. For example, if one person is feeling upset, the other person may provide comfort and understanding, which can help regulate and soothe the distressed person's emotions.

Mirror neurons, on the other hand, are specialized cells in our brains that fire both when we perform an action *and* when we observe someone else performing the same action. They essentially "mirror" the actions and experiences of others, allowing us to understand and empathize with them.

In relationships, mirror neurons play a crucial role in understanding and connecting with one another. When we observe someone expressing an emotion, our mirror neurons activate, and we can feel that emotion ourselves to some extent. This helps us to empathize with the other person and understand what they are going through. It enables us to "mirror" their emotions and respond in a supportive and empathetic manner.

Simply put, co-regulation is about how we support and influence each other's emotions and behaviours in relationships. Mirror neurons, on the other hand, help us understand and connect with others by mirroring their actions and emotions in our own brains. Both concepts are important for building and maintaining healthy and empathetic relationships.

**In addition to providing emotional support, healthy relationships offer many other practical benefits.** Wouldn't you agree that having someone to rely on in times of need—whether it's for emotional support or practical assistance—can make a big difference in our lives? We all want to have that one person to call in times of stress and struggle. Whether it's a death in the family, trouble at work, a political crisis, or just an overload of stress, we all need to be able to tell ourselves, *"I am not alone in this; someone has my back."*

We're also more likely to succeed and achieve our goals when we have a strong support system of healthy relationships in place. Knowing we have some wonderful cheerleaders in our corner can enhance our life-long performance.

Now, healthy relationships aren't just beneficial for the individuals involved: they also benefit society as a whole. When we have positive relationships with others, we're more likely to contribute to our communities and create a more harmonious society. We learn compassion and understanding from each other, and we all want to be worthy of others' love and complete acceptance. So basically, the importance of healthy relationships cannot be overstated.

Having healthy relationships can help us learn to keep our other relationships healthy, too. In a study conducted by Creasey and Ladd in 2004[1], researchers explored the link between someone's attachment style—we'll get further into that later—their understanding of how to handle negative

---

1    Creasey, G. and A. Ladd. "Negative mood regulation expectancies and conflict behaviors in late adolescent college student romantic relationships: The moderating role of generalized attachment representations," *Journal of Research on Adolescence*, 14(2), 2004. pp. 235–255. Available at: https://doi.org/10.1111/j.1532-7795.2004.01402005.x.

emotions, and how they behave in relationship conflicts. No relationship is always perfect—however, when trouble does arrive, it's the people who feel secure in their relationships who can navigate it the best. Having good attachments can help us manage conflicts in a healthy way.

### Healthy Relationships and Technology

In the chapters that follow, we'll delve deeper into the specific components of healthy relationships and offer practical strategies for building and maintaining them in a world increasingly dominated by what happens online. Our lifestyles have evolved and so have our relationships.

The modern-day consumer is quite smart, educated, and has access to tons of free relationship advice on social media (which is sometimes good, but often inaccurate or half-baked). We are being influenced—literally—to such a great extent that we are turning to TikTok, Twitter, Facebook, and Instagram (and many other social media outlets) to soothe us, give us answers, and offer solutions to the conflicts in our lives. And while some influencers and micro-celebrities do their best to avoid deceiving their audiences, most do not—and even the best-intentioned influencer ultimately prioritizes our engagement with their content over actually improving our lives. We all know that a little knowledge is a dangerous thing—if the picture is not complete, it doesn't truly make sense. Real relationships are complex and nuanced, but nuance and the For You page aren't best friends.

We live in an increasingly isolated world, where it can be easy to get our social interaction in soundbites instead of hugging our partners, engaging with each other, and having meaningful, heartfelt conversations. Until our genetic makeup is completely altered, it is paramount to have healthy relationships in our lives—and this quest is one of the existential crises of modern-day Homo *sapiens*.

**So, what does a healthy, adult romantic relationship look like?** Although it has many components, broadly speaking, it is one in which both partners feel secure, respected, and supported. Its foundation lies in honesty, trust and transparency. It involves continuous open communication, mutual understanding, and a willingness to work through conflicts and challenges together.

Since this has been an area of interest for me for a long time, I like to look around and try to see who embodies a strong and healthy relationship. I have admired Will Smith's work since the days of *The Fresh Prince of Bel-air* and was further impressed after watching *The Pursuit of Happiness*. To my therapist self (Ok, I might be slightly biased, as I already like those two) Will Smith and Jada Pinkett Smith come across as a secure powerful couple.

The couple married in 1997 and, as you can imagine, have faced many challenges and changes in their relationship. In an interview with Oprah Winfrey, Will Smith said, "Jada and I have always had a very honest relationship. We've always talked about everything. We've always been open. And that's the only way you can have a long-lasting relationship." Of course, at recent Oscar's night the entire world was talking about how Will punched Chris Rock for making a joke about Jada's hair loss. When he won Best Actor award, he tearfully likened his actions protecting his wife to the powerful sense of protection Richard Williams felt towards his family. He also apologized to the Academy of Motion Pictures (although not outwardly to Chris Rock—I sure hope this has been resolved between them).

Some fans have been cheering his fierce sense of familial honour and protection. A large segment of the audience, on the other hand, has been disappointed by his behaviour and considers it repugnant and disgraceful. We will leave it at that and won't dissect the incident more (though personally, I do not think violence is an answer when we become emotionally activated.)

Jada Pinkett Smith has also spoken about the importance of communication and compromise in their relationship, saying, "We've learned to really listen to each other, to really hear each other, and to really be there for each other in a way that I don't think either of us have ever experienced in any other relationship." The couple seems to respect each other, and their family looks lovely. To me, they appear to have a strong, secure attachment despite being in an open (non-monogamous) relationship in the past.

But let's look at a fictional example as well. I wasn't familiar with Milo and Cami from the show *The Ghost Club* until one of my clients informed me about them. Upon looking into their characters, I found that in "The Ghost Club," Milo and Cami are two high school students who form a strong bond after discovering they both have the ability to communicate with ghosts. Despite the challenges they face in their supernatural adventures, their relationship remains consistently supportive, trusting, and loving. Milo and Cami exhibit secure attachment by showing balance of independence and togetherness, trust, mutual respect, and open communication. Indeed, it is quite sweet.

I invite you to take a moment to reflect on your current relationship status. Quiet the external noise and give yourself a moment to evaluate your current relationships with clarity.

**Answer the questions that follow as honestly as you can:**
- Are you both able to express your thoughts and feelings freely? You probably know your answer—but do you know what your person feels?
- Are you able to negotiate and compromise on important issues?
- Is there mutual respect and a sense of equality?
- Are you both able to pursue your own interests and goals and contribute to shared vision?
- Do you feel comfortable being you (your true authentic self, not pretending) around your partner?

A healthy adult relationship has a generous dose of mutual appreciation and has a strong depth of connection. It has a blend of passion, intimacy, and friendship. Are these elements present in your relationships?

When counsellors work with our clients, it is about creating a corrective emotional experience for them: a pattern for a healthy emotional relationship that they can take with them outside the therapy room. Although therapy can be helpful, it may not be needed by everyone who struggling in relationships.

## *Hardship and Bonding*

A study published in the *Journal of Social and Personal Relationships*[2] found that people who went through a traumatic event together reported feeling a stronger sense of closeness and connection than those who did not share the experience. The study also found that the more severe the adversity, the greater the level of bonding that occurred.

---

2   Olff M. Bonding after trauma: on the role of social support and the oxytocin system in traumatic stress. Eur J Psychotraumatol. 2012;3. doi: 10.3402/ejpt.v3i0.18597. Epub 2012 Apr 27. PMID: 22893838; PMCID: PMC3402118.

While some people might become more isolated because of traumatic events, form negative thought patterns and beliefs, as well as can develop coping mechanisms that turn into their own problems later, sometimes, we learn important lessons during hard times in our lives.

**It happened for a couple I know, friends of my husband and I:**

*Jen and Dan had been together for 20 years and had faced their fair share of ups and downs. They met in their 20s, travelled the world, had children, saw a variety of gains and losses. They encountered everything from financial struggles to health issues, but always worked together to overcome whatever obstacles came their way. Sometimes they got help from their friends and family members, sometimes they saw their pastor, sometimes they took a sabbatical from the relationship and then got back together.*

*But even though they worked at it, their relationship was strained. You could often see them bickering and arguing over small things, and they had a hard time finding common ground and communicating effectively. Dan's sarcasm was a bit too much for Jen at times. As the years went by, they began to wonder if they would ever be able to strengthen their bond and truly be there for each other in the way they wanted to be.*

*At times, they would get close to other people in their lives— their primary emotional relationships were with other people who had their individual attention, rather than each other. They were starting to lose hope that things would ever change.*

*But then something unexpected happened. Jen was diagnosed with cancer, and suddenly everything else seemed to fade into the background. Dan was afraid to lose her completely and Jen was pushing him away. She was suffering, he was hurting, and the children were scared.*

*They started to have honest conversations, reminiscing about the good times, and what the future might look like. All of the petty arguments and misunderstandings that had once seemed so important suddenly seemed insignificant—Dan made an effort to be there for her, and Jen allowed that. In the face of this challenge, Jen and Dan realized that they needed each other more than ever.*

*As they navigated the ups and downs of Jen's treatment, they found that their bond had grown stronger than ever. They were able to support and understand each other in a way that they had never been able to before, because it was no longer about ego and distractions: it was about their emotions and what really mattered to them.*

*Eventually, Jen made a full recovery, and she and Dan were grateful for the new level of understanding and connection that they had reached. They knew that they had been through a lot together, but they also knew that they were stronger for it.*

**Would you like to do yourself a huge favour right now?** Now that you know how critical healthy emotional relationships are, make a promise to yourself to actively look for them. Ask the people around you to fulfill those needs that come with being a human being—there is no shame in admitting that we all require love.

The best thing you can do for yourself is provide yourself with true, authentic, and genuinely caring relationships, while running far away from venomous people. While we cannot choose our families, we can use our discernment to decide who we allow in our adult lives. You get to shape your world with the people who will help you complete your life journey successfully.

Human bonding can be hard to understand, yet simple enough to navigate—if we take off all the masks, put aside our egos and the myths we've been fed, and consider the science behind it all, we can greatly improve our chances at healthy and happy relationships.

# CHAPTER 2

## Left On Read

### Attachment styles and technology

Much has been said and written about attachment styles[3], but since it is one of the foundations on which many of our key points are based, I'll quickly touch on them here.

Childhood attachment styles often influence the quality of our adult romantic relationships. When I interact with a new client, I want to understand how they were raised, how their relationships were with their caretakers. I want to identify the adjectives they use to describe their parents, family members, and authority figures. This information gives me insight into their attachment style and allows me to much more to accurately assess where they are in their relationships journeys now.

The quality of our relationships growing up has such a profound impact on our adult attachment styles. A little information about a client's childhood can give clinicians an insight into our clients' patterns and suggest what could be happening our clients' current relationships.

---

3   To dive deep into attachment styles and how they affect your life, I would recommend the works of Sue Johnson, John Bowlby, and Amir Levine and Rachel Heller.

Simply put, attachment styles refer to the patterns of behaviour that people display in their relationships with others. These patterns are said to be largely influenced by the early experiences of a newborn with their caregivers and can have a lasting impact on an individual's relationships throughout their life. The ways in which a child relates to and interacts with others, particularly in close relationships, becomes their attachment style. These attachment styles can ultimately affect how people relate to and interact with their romantic partners, with their colleagues, with authority figures, and many other crucial relationships. However, our upbringing isn't the only thing that creates our personalities later in life: there is a genetic component, and our environment influences our social personality too.

Many things in our lives are ever-changing and temporary, and similarly, attachment styles are not fixed. Trauma can leave us struggling to trust, or positive experiences can help us feel more secure and grounded in our relationships.

When I discuss attachment styles with folx I work with, I ask them to take in this information with an open mind, without judging or assigning labels to different styles. I remind them that all individuals can form healthy and fulfilling relationships. If there is a buy-in from everyone involved, the work of healing and moving forward becomes much easier.

So, what is your attachment style? If you are clear on this—amazing, well done! You are way ahead of the curve. If not, read on, and let's navigate the world of connection, human behaviour, and bonding together.

### *The Four Attachment Styles*

**Secure attachment style.** Individuals with a secure attachment style are comfortable with intimacy and are able to form close, trusting relationships. They are able to rely on their caregivers for support and feel confident in their ability to handle challenges. They are able to communicate openly and honestly with their partners, and they are able to balance their own needs with the needs of their partners. They could possess some emotional intelligence. People with secure attachments can handle conflict well or learn how to deal with it, and are aware when their relationship needs a reset, recharge, or upgrade.

Let's take an example from a history class. The Roman Republic and the Aetolian League were both independent city-states in ancient Greece, and in 3rd century BCE, they formed an alliance in order to strengthen their military and diplomatic power. This partnership enabled both parties to defend against external threats and achieve their shared goals.

The alliance was based on mutual respect and cooperation, and it was characterized by a high level of trust and loyalty. Both sides honoured their commitments to one another and worked together to resolve conflicts and differences. If the Roman Republic and Aetolian League were a couple, they'd definitely have a secure partnership.

This book explores a few tricks for creating that kind of fulfilling, mutually beneficial relationship—especially when life seems to become lonely and monotonous.

**Anxious-preoccupied attachment style**. People with an anxious-preoccupied attachment style often worry about being abandoned or rejected, and they may have a harder time trusting their partners. They may be clingier or more demanding in their relationships, and they may have a harder time with emotional intimacy. They could be thinking, *if I am vulnerable with my partner, will they meet my demand or mock me?*

Someone with an anxious-preoccupied style could be holding onto many negative beliefs about themselves. They typically have a strong need for reassurance and may struggle with trust. They may also have difficulty regulating their emotions, and their anxiety or insecurity in their relationships can drive their partners away. We've seen cases where anxiety in a conflict leads to someone shutting down and emotionally stonewalling their partner.

**Dismissive-avoidant attachment style**. People with a dismissive-avoidant attachment style tend to prioritize their own independence and may have a harder time with intimacy and emotional closeness. They may downplay the importance of close relationships and may have difficulty with emotional expression. They may also find it challenging to rely on others for support and may have a hard time seeking help when needed. They might say they are fine when they are not, denying their basic need for connection and love.

People with dismissive-avoidant attachments may have a tendency to push their partners away or to minimize their own emotions in order to avoid vulnerability. They have dealt with many challenges in life on their own and now claim not to need the supportive other. Continuous self-reliance and not asking for help when they need it can lead to exhaustion or burnout. People with a dismissive-avoidant attachment style could very well blame these feelings on their partner when they never expressed their needs in the first place.

**Fearful-avoidant attachment style**. Individuals with a fearful-avoidant attachment style may have a negative view of themselves and may feel unworthy of love and affection. They may have a hard time trusting others and may feel uncomfortable with intimacy.

People with a fearful-avoidant attachment style may feel torn between their desire for closeness and their fear of being rejected or abandoned, and thus avoid intimacy all together. This internal turmoil, whether conscious or subconscious, could be painful.

**Attachment styles are not set in stone.** I often have folks sharing the results of their attachment styles—if they're not secure, some of them tend to think that their relationships are doomed to fail. I remind them that attachment styles are not fixed. They can certainly change over time due to healthy interactions, new relationships, increasing self-awareness, and the influence of the world we live in.

Individuals may exhibit traits of multiple attachment styles, and it is not uncommon for someone's attachment style to shift over the course of their life—or for them to exhibit different styles with different people in their lives.

Folks, if you understand yourself really well—we all have blind spots, but with work we can get to know ourselves—it might be easier to understand your partner and be emotionally attuned to their needs and your own. It's important for both partners to be aware of their own attachment styles and how this might be affecting their relationship. It can be helpful for couples to discuss and understand each other's attachment styles and work together to find ways to support and strengthen their relationship.

Sometimes it takes a rough patch to get a couple to put that work in, while other times couples are proactive and want to shore up their relationship against trouble.

## *Attachment and Technology*

Attachment styles can interact with technology in complex ways. Imagine you are at a busy airport, a coffee shop, or a playground. You notice a mother and a toddler. Mother is busy on her phone—texting, emailing, or talking to someone while the toddler is tugging at mother's clothes to get her attention. Mother says, "Go play, you are fine," but continues to stay engaged in whatever she is doing.

We are not judging the mother at all: perhaps she is paying a bill or dealing with an emergency, responding to work messages, or just using her phone to decompress. But, if this is a habit, what kind of message is she sending the child? What do you think this child starts to believe about themself? If this continues to happen on a regular basis, the child might end up feeling, *I am not important, no one cares, I must take care of myself, I must not bother mommy*—many different narratives can form in this little child's brain, which can affect their attachment style growing up.

On the other hand, if the mother is in awe of what the child is doing and where they are trying to draw his attention, it can form a wonderful connection between the two. Technology can impact existing relationships, and this can affect attachment patterns. For example, excessive use of technology can interrupt face-to-face interactions, which can weaken emotional bonds between partners, friends, or family members.

Technology can also create new opportunities for forming relationships and social connections, which can also impact attachment patterns. For example, social media and online dating platforms have made it easier for people to meet and connect with others, potentially leading to new romantic relationships. However, technology can provide new opportunities for people to engage in infidelity or other forms of relationship betrayal, leading to attachment-related issues such as mistrust and insecurity.

Research suggests that individuals with different attachment styles may be affected differently by technology. For example, those with anxious-preoccupied attachments may be more likely to use technology to seek reassurance and attention from their partners, while those with avoidant attachments may use technology to avoid intimacy and maintain emotional distance.

**I once had a traditional, monogamous couple in therapy[4] who displayed this difference well:**

*Kathy and Matt had been together for six years. Kathy had a secure attachment style, which meant she was comfortable with intimacy and trust and was able to balance her own needs with those of her partner. Matt, on the other hand, had an anxious-preoccupied attachment style. He often worried about being abandoned or rejected, and he had a harder time trusting Kathy.*

*At first, Kathy didn't think Matt's attachment style was a problem. To be frank, she did not even know much about attachment. She thought it was sweet that he cared so much about their relationship and wanted to spend as much time together as possible. She didn't mind him texting multiple times a day. This worked well for her in the honeymoon phase of the relationship.*

*But as time went on, she started to feel overwhelmed by his constant need for reassurance and affection. She found herself feeling resentful and frustrated, and she started to pull away from him. I remember her telling me that she felt suffocated in the relationship and needed a break or some space from her partner. Texts that were adorable in the beginning were now annoying.*

*Matt noticed the change in Kathy's behaviour and became even more anxious. He started to push her even harder for affection and attention, which only made things worse. Kathy felt like she was losing herself in the relationship and began to distance herself even more. She looked forward to girl trips and work outings, which made Matt feel that Kathy's priorities were elsewhere.*

*When Kathy and Matt came to therapy, they were both unaware of the root cause of their issues. The couple eventually realized*

---

4    Names have been changed to protect their privacy.

*that they needed to address their different attachment styles and needed to examine their unmet attachment needs if they wanted to save their relationship.*

*This was all done in an experiential way—by really observing what was happening in the therapy room and what they were experiencing moment by moment. Therapy doesn't fix it all, of course. Therapists usually work as a process, a relationship consultant, so that couples can arrive at their own conclusion based on their feelings.*

*Kathy and Matt have been working on understanding each other based on their unique attachment styles and have been able to build a stronger, more resilient relationship that has been able to withstand the challenges of COVID-19 and continuous reassurance-seeking by Matt.*

## Using Your Attachment Style

Once you know your attachment style, you can understand your behaviour in relationships with more clarity. Your loved ones can possibly provide insight about how they perceive you. Gather feedback from your significant other and voila, you can learn to understand what you may need in a relationship to feel secure and connected to others.

If you have a secure attachment style, you may find it easier to form close, trusting relationships and may not have as much difficulty with emotional expression and communication. You may also feel more comfortable seeking support from others and may have an easier time trusting and relying on your loved ones. How about giving yourself an opportunity to connect with someone at a deeper level? Would you consider, getting off your phone, not choosing to swipe left and right and using your true personality and confidence to find your perfect match.

If you have an anxious-preoccupied attachment style, you can benefit from building trust in your relationships (this can be hard if you have been burned before). Learning how to regulate your emotions can be difficult work, but it's totally worth it—emotional regulation skills come with a lot of benefits in life and in relationships.

It can be quite helpful to practise self-soothing techniques. By developing your tool kit of coping mechanisms, you can manage your anxiety and develop a sense of self-worth and independence. When we can self-regulate (when we have tools to self-soothe and manage our emotions) then we can tap into the power of our mirror neurons and use co-regulation strategies to de-escalate our emotionally charged interactions.

If you have a dismissive-avoidant attachment style, you may benefit from working on becoming more open to intimacy and emotional expression. It may be helpful to practise being vulnerable and seeking support from others, as well as learning to rely on others—in the real world—for help when needed. Using the anonymity of the internet to avoid being perceived when you need something can be tempting, but it's emotional honesty in your relationships that will help you feel truly cared for. Start by taking small risks of vulnerability in your relationships and see what happens. Being vulnerable is not necessarily a bad thing. It's good to be self-reliant, but everyone could use some help and assistance from time to time.

If you have a fearful-avoidant attachment style, you may benefit from working on building trust and self-worth in your relationships. Just like anxious-preoccupied folks, this group can get a lot out of becoming super clear in their communication and asking for reassurance as required.

However, it's also important to develop your own self-management tools and discernment—sometimes, you need your partner, but sometimes you need to lean in and connect with yourself. Ask yourself—*who and what am I afraid of?* I recall once asking a client what prevents them from connecting with people, they are dating, and they said "Nothing," but after another moment they said, "My fear is that I will end up alone."

It can feel empowering to recognize our deep-rooted fears, to develop positive cognitions and build a strong sense of self-worth. That work can lead to a better life, being independent and taking care of some of our own needs while also trusting others and learning to exist in harmony with them—IRL[5].

As discussed earlier, attachment styles are not permanent and can evolve over time. It is absolutely possible to work on improving your attachment

---

5    "In real life."

style and developing healthier, more fulfilling relationships with your significant others. This may involve seeking therapy or support from a trusted professional, or practising self-reflection and self-awareness. It could also simply be a matter of finding an emotionally intelligent partner who helps you become the best version of yourself.

Oh, if only we were all so lucky, to have all our stars aligned—or perhaps if only restarting our lives was like updating an app or upgrading our phone.

# CHAPTER 3

——

# /Gen

## The art of open communication

No matter how well someone knows us, they are not a mind reader, and nor should they have to play guessing games. We do not deserve to be misunderstood, but getting good at understanding ourselves and expressing our needs requires practise and solid work. This foundation is either laid in our childhood by emotionally intelligent caregivers, or by the environment in which we grow up.

It is also possible that, at some later point in our lives, we become aware of our internal pain. We work on ways to overcome this emotional pain by developing patterns of behaviour to protect us from it—which might be avoidant, resistance-based, or overly expressive. A few of us have the insight to be clearly aware of our needs, to articulate them to our partners without beating around the bush. So, ask yourself: do you say what you feel to the people you love?

**Here is a situation I once found myself in, where I struggled to communicate openly:**

One time, I had told my husband we needed to go for dinner on Saturday and that he should pick a nice place. He delayed taking action. I was upset and under external stress and asked him a couple days later if he had made reservations. He said no, but he was looking into it.

In my fury, I said a bunch of different things. "I am too busy to go anyways." "No, wait a minute, I am no longer available and may have plans with my friends." "Hold on, I am actually too tired and want to just stay home, rest and relax."

My poor husband was confused, and asked me, "What do you actually want?"

Underneath all that chaos, I felt he was too busy, that he did not make me a priority, and that he was leaving things to the last minute. Truly, I wanted to go out; I was just upset that there was no clear plan around it.

*Phew!* This internal conflict and chaos of mine was disrupting our communication. I hear narratives like this too often from my clients. They can play out in a variety of different ways—One partner gets upset and screams or yells—In this case, me, and I am clearly not proud of it. In response, the other partner can shut down (creating a communication breakdown) yell back (escalating the situation with a fight response) or be left feeling confused.

On the other hand, when two people are able to see these patterns clearly and work together on identifying the real issues behind their communication breakdowns, their communication improves.

### Open Communication

Open communication in relationships allows for the free exchange of thoughts, feelings, and ideas between individuals. If you constantly feel that you are walking on eggshells around someone and that they could blow up any minute, if you have no clue what will disturb them, then something is truly off and needs immediate attention. Allow yourself to dig deep with your partner to get to the root cause of the issues, and work beyond your egos to strengthen your communication abilities. Through open communication we can build trust and understanding, which leads to a sense of connection and intimacy. There is something deeply attractive about knowing that you are desired and wanted, and that you have a wonderful person beside you to support you in your life journey.

When individuals are able to communicate openly and honestly, they are able to better understand each other's needs, can connect on common values, and can appreciate each other's boundaries, which can help to prevent misunderstandings and conflicts. Does your person know your non-negotiables? Do you know theirs?

Using social media to discuss urgent matters and vital issues can sometimes lead to misinterpretation or misrepresentation of good intentions, because the other party cannot see your emotions or body language.

Of course, there is also frequently a performative nature to publicly visible fights. I know of couples who fight on their social media pages, counting likes from their friends as wins—and others who feel backed into a corner and don't want to publicly admit they're wrong. Do you want people to take sides when you argue? If you silently nodded yes, you know there is an issue. Playing games and wanting to win isn't good for the quality of your bond in the long run.

Hold your partner's hand, know what's in your heart and speak your mind clearly rather than hiding behind technology to resolve painful experiences. Coming from a place of authenticity, speaking your truth with vulnerability has better chance of success rather than getting likes and nods of others. Of course, if bringing things up is not going to lead anywhere (i.e., if you've had the same conversation in the past and are feeling unheard or invalidated), we can use technology as a tool to keep the lines of communication open—but I would recommend finishing it in person (or at least privately). There's a lower chance of misunderstandings and higher rate of success through open dialogue and clearly understanding your person's perspective.

When people feel heard and understood, they are more likely to feel valued and supported by their loved ones. This can help to create a sense of emotional safety in a relationship, which is essential for building trust and intimacy.

I am sure many of my colleagues will agree that in a therapeutic setting, we often hear one of the partners saying that they do not feel heard or understood, that their feelings are being undermined and emotions not validated. Clearly, there is some sort of communication hurdle in these relationships—and any communication hurdle is easier to overcome when we work together with the person as opposed to overthinking it on our own.

**Here's a great example of a couple who worked together to solve a communication breakdown:**

*I once worked with a couple in which one partner was stronger and bulkier. When he got mad, she would feel unsafe. She had been treated poorly by her own father—he would get mad, and she as a child would shut down and would struggle to get her words out.*

*Interestingly enough, her partner did not have a clue. He'd never intended to scare her and didn't understand why she was shutting down. Once he realized that his demeanour was affecting her sense of safety, he made a conscious effort to self-regulate, remove himself from the physical space, and then reconnect with her to assure her they could overcome their marital challenges together.*

Such endings are heartwarming and make me feel proud of the work we do as couples' therapists—but I give all the credit to the partners for understanding each other's needs, and for being open to discussions around how to move forward. Emotion-focused therapists are simply process consultants for a relationship in trouble.

When parties are willing to engage in open communication, it can help resolve conflicts and work through challenges in a relationship. By being open and honest about their feelings and needs, individuals can work together to find solutions and move past any issues that may arise.

**Let's look at another great example of a celebrity couple.** Lee Byung-Hun and Lee Min-Jung is a South Korean celebrity couple who married in 2013. They have both had successful careers as actors and have had to navigate the challenges that come with being in the public eye.

Despite their busy schedules, the couple has always made an effort to prioritize their relationship and to communicate openly and honestly with each other. In an interview, Lee Byung-Hun said, "I think the most important thing for a couple is honesty. If you have honest feelings towards each other, you can overcome any obstacle."

Lee Min-Jung has also spoken about the importance of compromise and understanding in their relationship, saying, "We try to understand each other's schedules and work together to find a balance." Through their honesty, communication, and willingness to accommodate each other's busy lives, Lee Byung-Hun and Lee Min-Jung have been able to navigate their personal and professional life successfully, showing the world as to how to maintain a strong and loving relationship.

Not all couples are able to have open communication, even with help. I have had scenarios where one partner refuses to show up for therapy or is not willing to communicate, or where folks are stuck in a blame game and do not take accountability for their own actions or see their own patterns. This gives me a minor heartache, but it comes with the territory.

### *Communication Tools*

One of the most commonly asked questions I get when I tell someone that I am a couples' therapist is about practical tools to improve communication with your partner. Communicating doesn't come naturally to many of us. A lot of it has to do with who we are, how we were raised, and what kind of environment shaped us; but, like so many other things in life, communication can be learned and taught.

I am always amazed and in awe of couples who, even after being married for a long time or having known each other since high school, are together, deeply connected, and make each other feel special. These folx have discovered ways to prioritize each other and have experienced the deep satisfaction and eternal love that comes from having a solid emotional bond.

Even though happy, healthy couples do fight, they know how to turn towards each other later on, talk, and resolve the differences instead of brushing things under the carpet. They, in some ways, have mastered the art of communicating well. You both deserve a sense of safety, good laughs, and good times—and those experiences can leave a lasting impression on our psyches. So here are a few tools to help you build that special bond.

**Set aside dedicated time for communication.** Make time to regularly sit down and have open and honest conversations with your partner. This can be a specific time each week or a daily check-in to discuss any issues or concerns. Have an emotion wheel with you—a print out, or you can pull it up on a screen— and dive deep into those emotion-based conversations. Share your thoughts and feelings with your partner (and distinguish between the two), even if they may be difficult to discuss. It's important to be honest and open in your communication to build trust and understanding in the relationship.

**Practice active listening.** When your partner is speaking, give them your full attention and try to understand their perspective. Repeat back what they said to show that you heard and understood them.

**Use "I" statements.** When expressing your own feelings or concerns, use "I" statements to describe your own emotions and experiences, rather than placing blame on your partner. This can help to avoid defensiveness and encourage open communication.

**Seek help if it's needed.** If you're having difficulty communicating with your partner or if there are deeper issues impacting your relationship, it may be helpful to seek the guidance of a therapist or counsellor. They can provide support and help you learn effective communication skills.

**I still remember Tom and Sarah, who learned the importance of good communication when they had their first child:**

> *They had been together for five years but had been struggling to communicate effectively since after the birth of their baby. Tom often felt unheard and misunderstood, while Sarah felt like Tom wasn't open and honest with her.*

> *Sarah felt Tom was spending too much time at the office and gaming with his friends. She felt like he was working too late, not putting in enough effort into parenting their baby. Meanwhile, Tom felt Sarah was giving all the attention to the baby and that his needs were being neglected. Whenever he tried to talk to Sarah, she was too tired to connect or just asked him to do chores. When they connected with the clinic, they realized their maladaptive patterns.*

> *These behaviours that were not helping the situation—instead, they were causing the couple to lose their connection with each*

*other. Through therapy, they learned about the importance of active listening and expressing their own feelings using "I" statements.*

*Every therapist has to do their own work to work through their relationship demons and make safe and effective use of self in therapy, so I'll sometimes share tidbits of my own life. In my early twenties, my interactions with my partner were a lot like Tom and Sarah's. What did he do wrong or didn't do at all? "You watch tv all night long, you play too many video games." I had to learn to say, "I feel unloved" or "I feel lost."*

*Tom and Sarah also learned the art of emotional attunement (yes, it absolutely can be learned) and recognized that the struggles they were facing were quite common with new parents. They had to be there for each other and take care of this new being who had entered their world.*

*Tom and Sarah made a commitment to set aside dedicated time each week to have open and honest conversations with each other. They practised active listening and made an effort to understand each other's perspectives as well as emotions. They also worked on using "I" statements to express their own emotions and needs, rather than placing blame on the other person. Sarah was open to physically connecting with Tom again, and he was willing to become more present as a father. Of course, they fall off the wagon every so often and need a tune-up session, but they are still together and doing well.*

If you want to upgrade your relationship, own your part in it and see what you can do to improve communication with your partner. Relationships become stronger when open and positive communication is a norm and a non negotiable . It's one of the stepping stones to building trust, understanding, and intimacy, and it helps foster a sense of emotional safety and support.

# CHAPTER 4

## Cross-Platform Play

### Conflict resolution and navigating differences

The word conflict itself can be nerve-wracking, but conflict is part and parcel of our everyday lives. Healthy couples fight, too. The difference is whether or not they know how to resolve conflicts successfully, and if they can accommodate each other's points of view.

Like I mentioned in chapter one, secure folks are better at resolving conflicts—even when those conflicts stress them out. What do you do when faced with conflict? Do you fight or shut down? Do you run away from problems or shove them under the carpet?

Someone once asked me about my conflict-resolution techniques. If I am being completely honest, I have probably avoided issues that needed resolution, or prayed that they would disappear and not need to be addressed. My wiser side today will talk to my younger self and say, "girl, small issues, when not addressed, can *become* big." To make my marriage work, I had to learn ways in which my partner would listen. We had to upgrade our communication game to find ways to navigate our differences and solutions that worked for both of us. It's still something we have to work on from time to time. Small conflicts—when left unresolved—can lead to big feelings of resentment and frustration.

We can set ourselves up for maladaptive patterns by avoiding difficult conversations. Someone who avoids conflict will agree to whatever they think will prevent a fight and will pretend not to be hurt or bothered by something while keeping their true feelings hidden inside.

When it comes to my own conflicts, how I react is contextual. Many times, in the past, the person I was interacting with was dysregulated and I spun out of my window of tolerance and became dysregulated myself. The win is if they are dysregulated, and I can co-regulate them by staying in my window of tolerance—not becoming anxious (which clinicians call hyperarousal) or shutting down (hypo-arousal).

So, were you given the tools of self-regulation when you were young? Perhaps some of us were, and some did not get the memo. Can you say confidently that you got the support of co-regulation from an elder, caretaker or wise person in your life?

Based on their past experiences, many folks who come and see me tell me they do not like conflict and would rather not argue. They comply. On the other hand, many feisty ones tell me, "I am not the one to back down"—but this constant bickering and fighting doesn't serve our relationships either. Can you see the way that some people are stuck in shutdown mode and some in flight? We need to find some kind of middle ground and perhaps eventually find our ventral vagal state. Think of this as feeling sunny inside or imagine it like you are driving on a warm beautiful sunny day; the ventral vagal state is when your nervous system is calm and centred, and you don't feel threatened. That's when you can really think.

We can all hugely benefit from an appropriate way to resolve difficult situations. Right now, at this moment, I invite you to take a deep breath and see if there is any shift in your internal state. Now see if you can implement some of these strategies to resolve conflicts in a healthy and effective way.

**Take a step back and calm down.** It's important to take a moment to calm down and regulate your emotions before attempting to resolve a conflict. This can help prevent things from escalating and allow you to approach the situation more rationally.

Someone once told me—or perhaps I read it somewhere—that no resolution can be achieved when two parties are heated. We need to deal with anger first (and the host of other emotions it brings with it, like bitterness, aggression, humiliation, betrayal, hostility, and skepticism) before finding an actual resolution for the problem.

**Listen actively.** It's important to really listen to your partner and try to understand their perspective. Avoid interrupting or getting defensive, and instead try to really hear what they have to say. See if you can pick on the emotions underneath their words.

If one partner says, "You never take the trash out!" Do they mean they are exhausted? Are they stressed? Are they under a work deadline? Are they dealing with a friend's cancer news, or do they simply want you to acknowledge that you could be doing more? What are the feelings under the words? Where are those feelings coming from? And if a person is having a certain feeling, what does it say about them?

There's a lot in here, so let it simmer for a bit, or come revisit this again and again until you master the art of active listening.

**Communicate openly and honestly.** Be honest about your feelings and needs and try to express them in a clear and respectful way. Avoid criticism or blame, and instead focus on finding a solution that works for both of you. If we can step out of blame and defensiveness, we do a huge favour to ourselves and our relationships.

**Seek compromise.** In any conflict, it's important to find a solution that works for both parties. This may involve making compromises and finding a middle ground. It's ok to give and take.

**Seek outside help if necessary.** If you're having trouble resolving conflicts on your own, it can be helpful to involve a therapist or a counsellor who understands relationship dynamics. These people can provide unbiased support and guidance to help you and your partner find healthy ways to communicate and resolve conflicts.

**Here's an example of how I've seen a well-handled fight play out:**

*John and Sarah are having a conflict over household chores. John feels like Sarah isn't pulling her weight and is always leaving a mess for him to clean up. Sarah feels like John is being overly critical and not taking into account the fact that she works full-time, struggles with ADHD, and has other responsibilities.*

*To resolve this conflict, they might start by taking a moment to calm down and regulate their emotions. John has to be less critical, more compassionate and Sarah has to get better at time management, prioritize, and remind John that they are in it together.*

*They can listen actively to each other's perspective, tap into their person's emotions, and try to understand where the other is coming from. They can discuss their feelings and needs, their wants and wishes, and seek compromise by finding a way to divide the household chores in a way that works for both of them.*

*They might have to hire a cleaner, invest in a babysitter, or find time to make cleaning a fun chore to do together to save their relationship.*

## Navigating Differences

Differences—in core values, personalities, around parenting, culture, family, and politics—can be challenging for some relationships. But differences can also open us up to a whole new world.

Differences are a natural part of any relationship and should be celebrated. At times, they might make communication difficult, or hinder a bond—if they do, they need to be explored. By understanding your differences, you and your partners can find ways to work through them, and some mutually agreed-upon rules can be established so that your relationship works out smoothly.

**Invite curiosity and compassion into your communication.** Be curious about your partner's differences and how they shape them. Celebrate these differences and know it's ok to disagree on some matters. Communicate openly and honestly how you feel about your differences—take the time to listen to your partner's perspective and share your own. Be willing to have difficult conversations, when necessary, but add a healthy measure of compassion and kindness to them.

**Practice empathy often:** How would you like to be treated if you were in your partner's shoes? This perspective might allow you to be open minded and understand where the other person is coming from. This can be a valuable addition to your capacity to understand and connect with your partner. You'll be surprised to know how many times my colleagues and I hear "I just don't understand my partner."

**Focus on common ground and shared values.** While it's important to acknowledge and respect differences, it can also be helpful to focus on the things that bring you and your partner together. This can help to create a sense of unity and connection, even while celebrating your differences. What was it about your partner that drew you to them in the initial phases of the relationship?

**Practice compromise and become friends with patience.** It is ok to be accommodating and to compromise and adjust. Is the battle worth fighting for? Is there any scope for flexibility and finding ways to let go of things that don't matter in the grand scheme of things? Leaving the toilet seat up or down can surely be annoying, there could be disagreements over which genre of movies to watch or what new food to try, but as long as there is mutual respect and willingness to support each other these disagreements and differences can be worked through.

Give some of these strategies a try and see if your relationship feels fresh and rejuvenated. It might involve some trial and error but stick to the plan and work with each other to invite compassion, curiosity, effort, empathy, and willingness to accommodate your partner's needs and desires into your relationship.

**Here's a couple I know who were able to work through their differences:**

*Samantha and John had been together for five years and were very much in love. However, they had always had their differences and it seemed like they were constantly arguing about something. Some days John would say Sam was too high maintenance, and that nothing made her happy. Samantha often questioned "Does he not want kids with me?" or "Does he not want kids' period?" Many times, they would disagree on what to do together on the weekends.*

*They were getting tired of the constant bickering and wanted to find a way to navigate their differences more successfully. They* tried sitting down and having a heart-to-heart conversation about their relationship and what was important to each of them. They found common ground in their love for music and long drives.

During one of the conversations, they realized that they simply had to accept who the other person actually was and not who each wanted the other person to be. Their communication styles were different— Samantha tended to be more emotional and reactive while John was more logical and analytical. This was often the root cause of their misunderstandings, but they still loved and cared about each other.

They learned to listen to each other more carefully and to try to understand where the other person was coming from. Instead of arguing, they talked about how they felt and how they could make things work for both of them. Finally, the real issues were getting attention: John wanted more time to be ready to be a father, while Samantha was concerned about her biological clock.

Both decided to give themselves six more months to see if they could make it work—and make it work they did. They made an effort to compromise more and to find solutions that could work for both of them. To alleviate John's fears around being a father, they considered possibly starting with a fur baby.

They also made sure to plan a little "me time" for each of them. If John wanted to go out with his friends on a Saturday night, Samantha said she did not mind, as long as they made plans to do something together on Sunday. John encouraged Sam to restart her once a month "Wine Wednesdays" that she had relished before the start of the pandemic.

Over time, I noticed their relationship become much more harmonious. They were able to navigate some of their differences *more successfully and found ways to often become emotionally attuned to each other. By having some "me time" planned, they were able to enjoy each other's company and support each other in their individual pursuits. They clearly knew that they were not perfect, and both had their shortcomings, but they were committed to working together to build a strong and loving relationship, and to continue having tough conversations around their differences.*

I often think about Jay-Z and Beyoncé, who have a long history of navigating their differences successfully. Jay-Z and Beyoncé have been married since 2008 and have faced their fair share of challenges and controversies over the years. It is wonderful to see their consistent efforts to support each other. They often seem to demonstrate their commitment to each other and very much seem to be in love. Do you recall when they released their joint album "Everything Is Love", showcasing their united front as a couple? The album's lyrics and themes celebrated their journey together, emphasizing forgiveness, growth, and the strength of their bond. It served as a testament to their commitment to each other and their ability to overcome challenges.

Beyond public performances and music, Jay-Z and Beyoncé have also shared glimpses of their love through social media. They are occasionally post affectionate photos and messages dedicated to each other, offering fans a peek into their personal lives, and reinforcing their deep emotional connection.

It was quite endearing to see that during Beyoncé's 2018 Coachella performance, which became known as "Beychella," Jay-Z surprised the audience by joining her on stage. As they performed together, their chemistry and love for each other were palpable. Towards the end of the performance, Jay-Z stood beside Beyoncé and gazed at her with admiration, showcasing a deep emotional connection between them. The moment was significant because it not only demonstrated their shared passion for music, but also symbolized their unwavering support for one another's careers.

In an interview with Oprah Winfrey, Beyoncé stated that she and Jay-Z have learned to communicate effectively with each other and have also made an effort to prioritize their relationship. They make time for each other, despite their busy schedules.

In a heart-melting interview with David Letterman, Jay-Z stated that "the best thing about marriage is the growth. You get to see someone at their worst, and you still love them. And they get to see you at your worst, and they still love you." He emphasized the importance of working through challenges and growing together as a couple.

Even Michelle Obama talks about seeing a therapist in her book *The Light We Carry*, to navigate relationship challenges with Barak. These couples serve as an inspiration to others who are working to strengthen their own relationships.

# CHAPTER 5

—

# (Verified)

## The importance of trust

*When a young couple—let's name them Jack and Emily—connected with me, they told me they had been together for a few years. They loved each other very much, but they had one major issue: they struggled with trust. There is almost always a history behind mistrust in a relationship, though some people are just less inclined to trust in general.*

*Here, there was a history: Jack had been betrayed in a previous relationship and it had left him feeling insecure, and hesitant to fully open up to Emily.*

*Emily, on the other hand, had always been a very trusting person, but she found it difficult to understand why Jack couldn't trust her. To show her love, she baked for him, took his clothes to the dry cleaners, and even invited Jack with her to company events.*

*But Emily's efforts to show him he was loved didn't get through Jack's difficulty trusting. Jack disliked when she talked to her male colleagues. When he'd had a few drinks, things usually became ugly—his fears of her leaving or finding someone else and his mistrust of the men around her turned into angry outbursts. Jack would typically apologize the next day or in a couple of days, but Emily started to become less and less open with him as she tried to avoid triggering what felt like sudden accusations.*

*Of course, Jack could see where she had been and what she had been up to on her social media. Sometimes, Jack would make sarcastic comments on her posts and photos. Being in that kind of relationship can be exhausting—though Emily was starting to become disheartened, she was afraid to breach the topic of Jack's insecurities.*

*Jack did not want to be a jealous boyfriend—let alone a frightening one—but he had to be open and honest about what he was feeling and how he was reacting. Although not quite stalking, Jack's obsession over Emily's social media profiles wasn't healthy for him or for their relationship.*

*They both acknowledged that trust was an important part of any relationship and that they needed to work on it together. Jack needed a lot of reassurance from Emily as he learned to let go of his anxieties and trust her more. Emily had to be more understanding and patient with Jack, and once he was honest about his fears instead of getting angry, she was able to do that. After all, she cared for him and his feelings.*

*Jack realized that trust was not something that he could build overnight, but rather that it was something that would take time and effort to cultivate.*

### Anxious Attachments and Trust

Does your partner continually need reassurance? This can be very exhausting, but not uncommon for folks who have anxious attachment styles. It could also be a sign of underlying insecurity or lack of trust in the relationship.

It's important to approach the issue with understanding and empathy and try to identify the root cause of your partner's need for reassurance. In some cases, the root cause lies outside the relationship, and the solution requires some solo work—I strongly believe that Jack in the above case could benefit from some individual therapy or support.

You can address your partner's insecurities through an open, compassionate dialogue—rather than through contempt, criticism or getting stuck in defence mode. Discuss your partner's concerns and insecurities and try to understand their perspective. You can also reassure your partner through actions, such as showing them additional love and affection, being consistent and reliable, and demonstrating your commitment to the relationship. Since every individual is unique, different things will work for different relationships.

It may be helpful to seek the advice of a therapist or a counsellor who can help you both work through any underlying issues and find healthy ways to address your partner's need for reassurance. Building and maintaining a healthy relationship requires effort, patience and understanding from both partners. Circumstances (or a dating app) might bring someone close to us, but it is up to us to nurture the relationship.

**Here's a couple who demonstrate both anxious and avoidant attachment styles, and how they work through the resulting imbalances:**

*Jane and John are a couple in which Jane is anxious while John is avoidant. This creates a dynamic where Jane feels like she is constantly seeking reassurance and affection from John, while John feels overwhelmed. He distances himself from Jane's need for constant reassurance and calls her "needy." She feels small for asking for her needs to be met in this relationship.*

*To overcome these differences and build a stronger bond, Jane has to be vulnerable with John about her insecurities and her feelings without being accusatory. John, in turn, has to be open, accepting, and willing to deliver what Jane needs.*

*It is not that John doesn't want to give, he just doesn't know how—they both care about each other and want to heal the rifts in their relationship, so they both have to take small risks to get closer to each other.*

*John might discover ways to show Jane affection and reassurance without feeling overwhelmed, and Jane might have to be more assertive in her communication without being aggressive or might have to learn when to back off and let John process her needs before reaching out to him again.*

*I believe it's their love and shared Catholic values that will allow Jane and John to work on their relationship and make an effort to understand and support each other, despite their different attachment styles making it difficult to get close.*

**And finally, here's a couple who both struggle to trust:**

*Sarah and Tom are a couple, and both of them are anxious in their relationship. This can lead to a dynamic where they are both constantly seeking reassurance and affection from each other, which can be overwhelming and exhausting for both of them.*

*They have to recognize this pattern, and in small consistent steps, find healthy ways to address their anxiety and communicate their needs to each other. Regular, open, and true conversations about their feelings and concerns are essential. Feeling heard and understood, and knowing they can be honest with each other, can reduce the need for constant reassurance.*

*It may also be helpful for Sarah and Tom to practice self-care and prioritize their own well-being. This can involve various adaptive coping mechanisms like exercise, relaxation techniques, and spending time with friends and family. Taking care of themselves can help them feel more grounded and confident in their relationship. When both Sarah and Tom are doing well individually, it's easier for them to turn towards each other and provide mutual support without needing constant reassurance.*

### *Practising Trust*

Many times, we'll do role playing—or, as some call them, *enactments*—in the therapy room This is a therapeutic technique where couples re-enact specific situations or conflicts from their relationship within the therapy session. The intent behind enactments is to provide a safe and structured environment for couples to better understand their patterns of communication, emotional dynamics, and underlying issues. They can help in

- **Promoting Awareness:** By observing and participating in these re-enactments, couples gain insight into how their actions, words, and emotions contribute to relationship dynamics.
- **Enhancing Communication:** By re-enacting conflicts or challenging situations, they can explore alternative ways of expressing themselves, listening, and understanding each other more effectively.
- **Building Empathy:** By stepping into each other's shoes and experiencing the situation from their partner's point of view, couples can gain a deeper appreciation for the emotions and motivations driving their behaviour.
- **Identifying Triggers and Patterns:** By observing these patterns in action, couples can recognize recurring themes or dynamics that contribute to their challenges, which opens the door for addressing them in therapy.
- **Working Through It:** Enactments also encourage emotional expression and facilitate problem solving.

Some couples find it amusing, some intriguing, and some, downright silly. What about you? Would you be up for something like that with your partner? Why not invite some playfulness in your relationship to refresh it, like a coat of fresh paint can add newness to an old, boring room?

Here's something you can try if you'd like. Be silly, be curious. Create your own script or use the ones I've got for you here. Slow down. Look into each other's eyes—giggle, laugh, and love each other unconditionally.

**1:**

I know we've had some trust issues in the past, but I really want to work on them and build a stronger, more trusting relationship.

*Here, partner 1 is making a bid for connection. It seems they want to work on their communication*

**2:**

I agree, trust is the foundation of a successful relationship. How do you think we can work on it?

*It's good news when the other person is open to this conversation. If they are busy, stressed out, or disengaged, this could look very different.*

### 1:

I think we should start by being more open and honest with each other. I know I haven't always been great about sharing my feelings and thoughts with you, and I want to work on that.

*A willingness to be more open is a good sign. But healing and personal development aren't linear: the next step to consider would be if 1 can keep this openness consistent.*

### 2:

I appreciate that. Thank you. What would you like from me? How can I support you in this?

*Using I statements is useful here. 2 also doesn't leave all the onus on 1: they ask how they can help. If you're in Person 2's shoes, the next step is to think "what do I need to do to make the situation better?"*

### 1:

Can you be more understanding and patient with me? It's very hard for me. I don't know how to trust, but I can try.

*This kind of difficulty with openness can very well be due to past trauma—Person 1 may not have shared the details yet, or even articulated them to themselves, but very few people live without some internal issue they're working on.*

### 2:

Absolutely. I'm willing to put in the effort as well. I am in it with you.

*This is one of the keys to working through issues together: a sense of "us against the problem" instead of "me against you."*

**1:**

It's easier not to be anxious when I know what is going on with you.

**2:**

I sometimes assume you know what's going on with me. I have to remind myself you are not a mind reader, and I have to let you know what bothers me instead of keeping quiet.

**1:**

I'm open to listening. I love you and I want to be able to trust you fully.

**2:**

I love you too, and I want to be with you. We rock and we are in this together.

You can see a few critical things happening here: a bid for connection that is answered, honesty about the struggles the couple is facing, and a sense of solidarity against those struggles.

**Being of Indian origin, I have to touch on one of my favourite Bollywood couples**—especially when trust seems so fragile in celebrity relationships. There are many celebrities Indian couples who have shared secrets of their relationship success, but nothing beats King Khan and his wife's love story.

Shah Rukh and Gauri Khan married in 1991. They have faced many challenges and changes in their relationship, including the demands of their careers and the attention of the media. When the entire nation is doting on your husband, it must be very hard for the wife to manage her insecurities and to continue to trust her partner. Shah Rukh has always made an effort to prioritize their relationship and is very open about it with the media.

In an interview with The Times of India, Shah Rukh Khan said, "Gauri and I have always had an open and honest relationship. We talk about everything and make sure we understand each other's needs and feelings. Communication is key in any relationship."

Gauri Khan has also spoken about the importance of compromise and understanding in their relationship, saying, "We try to understand each other's schedules and work together to find a balance. We know that we're not perfect and we're always learning and growing together."

They're certainly a prominent example of a successful and enduring Bollywood marriage. They have three children together and are known to be supportive of each other's careers. In the public eye it is clear that Shah Rukh and Gauri have a strong bond built on trust, mutual respect, and a deep commitment to their family and relationship.

# CHAPTER 6

—

# Drama DNI

## Setting and maintaining healthy boundaries

The thing with boundaries is that either we don't set them because we don't know how, or we are afraid to as we feel they won't be respected. If you have some non-negotiables, it is important to lay them on the table and to allow authenticity and truth to lead the conversation. You might be interested in inviting a romantic interest over for dinner—but you don't, because you are caught up in analysis paralysis, playing different scenarios in your head and trying to figure out how to avoid crossing the boundary your date doesn't know you have.

Many times, folks will have poor boundaries which are too loose. Maybe we're used to playing peacemaker within our families, trying to make sure everyone gets what they want (except for us). Imagine you are tired on a Friday night and just want to stay home and watch a movie, but your partner wants to go out. You agree, but you resent them deep down because come Sunday, you haven't reset or recharged. You overcommitted on the weekend.

On the other hand, sometimes we can be too rigid. If you always refuse to go with your partner when they ask you to meet their family, this can come off as deeply insensitive. Online, it's easy to ghost a person (drop them without a word) when life becomes too complicated. But relationships are about compromise, and mental rigidity at some point becomes unhealthy. Healthy boundaries might lie somewhere between two extremes.

Again, this could go back to how we were raised—were we conditioned to be nice rather than being honest? I know of folks who continue to stick together even when they know the relationship is over, because they are too afraid to say their truth and don't want to hurt the other person—even though they are miserable and know deep down the relationship will not work.

Within my own South Asian culture—which is collectivist—I have seen folks afraid to let go because they are wondering "what everyone thinks" rather than what they want or think. They might have children when they don't want to or stay in failed relationships to avoid the damage to their reputations.

## Practising Boundaries

Let's play out a scenario where you are trying to set a boundary and it is actually being respected—or your partner is trying to talk about what they need and want, and you acknowledge and value it.

**1:**

Hey, can we talk for a minute about something that's been on my mind?

**2:**

Sure, what's up?

**1:**

I've been feeling like we're not really respecting each other's boundaries lately. I feel like I'm always having to say no to things or drawing a line, and I don't like how you act out after that. You continue to push me.

**2:**

I had no idea you were feeling that way. I'm sorry if I've been crossing any boundaries. What can I do to help?

*This person is being kind and understanding. But the reaction could be different:*

**2:**

What are you talking about? You always get what you want? I have been nothing but patient and understanding.

*This is worth exploring further. If you are trying to be supportive, you have to listen, acknowledge, and take into account the emotions of your partner.*

**1:**

I think it would be helpful if we could set some clear boundaries and stick to them. For example, I really value my alone time and I feel like I haven't been getting enough of it lately. I need some space to recharge and have time to myself.

**2:**

I understand. I value your alone time too, and I'll make sure to respect that going forward. Is there anything else you'd like to set as a boundary?

*This person could accept it the boundary being set—they could also take accountability for their boundary-pushing and try to work on it.*

**2:**

I have always been a boundary pusher. This is new to me. I am going to work on that.

**1:**

I think it would also be helpful if we could establish some clear communication boundaries. I feel like I'm always being bombarded with calls and texts, and it's overwhelming. I need some time to process things and have space to think.

*Now, person 2 may not be aware person 1 was feeling overwhelmed—our partners aren't mind readers, after all, and if we struggle to set boundaries some of them might end up being news to the people we love.*

**2:**

Interesting. I thought I was showing I care.

*If you're on the receiving end of a boundary you didn't know you were crossing, it's important to be supportive of your partner for telling you, their needs.*

**2:**

I can definitely see how that would be overwhelming. I'll make sure to be more mindful of that going forward and give you the space you need. Come here, let me give you a hug. What else would you like to discuss?

**1:**

I think that's all for now. I just wanted to make sure we were on the same page and that we were both comfortable and respected each other. I love you and I want us to have a healthy, happy relationship.

**2:**

I love you too. I'm committed to us and working on being a better person. Not just for you but for myself. You don't have to bottle this up—I'll always do my best to listen when you tell me something's wrong.

I love when couples check in with each other regularly and make sure they're both feeling happy and fulfilled in the relationship or are working on preventing mishaps because they are diligent about it. Boundaries help to define the limits of what is and is not acceptable behaviour within the relationship, and they can help to protect both partners from feeling overwhelmed, taken advantage of, or disrespected.

**Here's the kind of thing that happens when boundaries are ignored:**

*Sarah has told Jim many times that when his brother yells at her, it triggers her. She'd like Jim to step up and have her back during those conversations rather than shutting down, avoiding it, keeping quiet, or saying "For the sake of family peace, let it go."*

*Jim says she is overreacting, that that's the way his brother is, or promises he will talk to him later. But this happening again and again is straining their relationship.*

## *Boundary Trouble*

When it comes to issues such as personal space (some people need to be alone to recharge and some people might get recharged in social settings), time (spending too much time with others and couple not getting enough time for themselves), and communication with extended family, it's essential to set some rules. For example, one partner may have a strong need for alone time, while the other may prefer to spend more time together.

When we work with blended families, boundary issues come up frequently. It is possible for a blended family struggling with boundary issues to overcome their toxic past and create a healthy and harmonious family dynamic, but it requires clarification as to who will play what role. How much do stepparents need to be involved in the lives of their partner's children? On the other hand, what is the role of biological parents outside of the blended family?

It may require a lot of work and effort from all family members to address and resolve any past issues, and it may also require family mediation and establishing fair, firm boundaries. Respectful, constructive communication is so needed in these situations, and it's important to seek an objective perspective as much as you can.

Setting boundaries around these issues can help to ensure that both partners feel heard and respected. A relationship with healthy boundaries allows both partners to feel more in control of their own lives and to establish a sense of mutual respect and understanding. When both partners know what to expect from each other, they can feel less anxious, which can lead to a stronger and more satisfying partnership.

CHAPTER 7

———

# Tag That, Please

## Emotional intelligence and really hearing our partners

Emotional intelligence, or the ability to recognize and understand one's own emotions and the emotions of others, can help create strong and healthy relationships. On the other hand, a lack of emotional intelligence can cause all kinds of problems.

Research indicates that having high emotional intelligence allows individuals to communicate effectively, resolve conflicts peacefully, and create a positive and supportive environment for themselves and their loved ones. Peter Salovey and John D. Mayer, who coined the term in 1990, stated that people who have developed emotional intelligence can "understand and express their own emotions, recognize emotions in others, regulate affect, and use moods and emotions to motivate adaptive behaviours." [6]

In romantic relationships, emotional intelligence can help partners understand and support each other's emotional needs. For example, if one partner is feeling overwhelmed and stressed, someone with high emotional

---

6    Peter Salovey, Mayer JD. Emotional intelligence. *Imagination, cognition and personality.* 1990 Mar;9(3): pp. 185-211.

intelligence may recognize this and offer comfort and support, rather than becoming reactive or argumentative and adding to the stress.

## *Validation*

Have you tried validating your partner's feelings recently? When we acknowledge and accept another person's feelings, even if we don't necessarily agree with or fully understand them, it can enhance our own capacity to be a better person. It involves showing empathy and communicating that you see and accept the person's emotions. This doesn't mean agreeing with everything your partner says—it just means hearing how they feel and taking their feelings seriously.

Validation—as opposed to dismissing other people's feelings—is a skill that needs practice and intention. If someone is talking to us and, say, we are clearly engrossed in a TikTok reel, it sends a message to them that they are not a priority. If it happens again and again, it can strengthen a certain neural pathway, change their beliefs about how we feel about them, and lead to disconnection. We are all letting technology and media control our attention spans and relationships.

After we have learned to attune to our person's emotions, validating those emotions enhances our connection with them. It helps to build a sense of security in a relationship by creating a sense of trust and connection between individuals. I know I am a priority when my partner puts away his phone and can sense my stress, frustration, sadness, or joy. When I am angry, annoyed, or upset, and my partner acknowledges it without judging or making assumptions, having his ear allows me space to process that emotion. When we feel that our emotions are understood and accepted by others, it can help us feel more supported and less alone.

Many times, our clients share that this safe space that their partners create for them when we work on emotional validation together is a new experience, that they'd never had that kind of validation in their life before. Validating your partner's emotions helps to reduce conflict and improve communication in a relationship.

When we trust our partners to take our feelings seriously, it's like our internal voice says, "I know I'll be understood so I can talk to you freely about this." We don't have to look for answers elsewhere or seek validation of our emotions beyond our partner to be accepted.

**Here are some ways you can practice emotional validation in your relationships:**

- **Listen actively.** Pay attention to what the other person is saying and show that you are listening by making eye contact, nodding, and offering verbal affirmations. You can repeat back what they are saying to make sure you understand and identify the underlying emotions.
- **Empathize.** Try to put yourself in the other person's shoes and understand their perspective. This can involve acknowledging the other person's feelings, even if you don't fully agree with them.
- **Communicate acceptance.** Use language that communicates that you see and accept the other person's emotions. For example, you might say "I can see that you are feeling upset about this," or "I understand that you are feeling frustrated," and don't add "but".
- **Practice mindfulness.** Be present in the moment and try to focus on the other person's emotions without getting distracted or reacting defensively. Do you think you can turn the TV off, put the phone away and just be there with your partner?

## *Emotional Invalidation*

In many unhealthy situations, I have seen one person being gaslit by the other. Gaslighting is a form of psychological manipulation in which someone attempts to make another person question their own reality, memories, or perceptions. This could be intentional (and if it is, you need to be out of that relationship) or it can be a reaction in the heat of the moment. If we are not aware that what we are doing is wrong, how can we change our behaviour?

**Can you identify what is going on between Michael and Rebecca here?**

### Michael:

I don't understand what you're talking about. I never said that.

### Rebecca:

Yes, you did. You said that I was overreacting and that I was being too sensitive.

**Michael:**

No, I didn't. You must be misremembering. You are putting words in my mouth. You're a drama queen.

**Rebecca:**

I know what I heard, Michael. You can't just deny it and try to manipulate me.

**Michael:**

I'm not though, Rebecca. I am trying to stay calm here. You're just being paranoid and exaggerating things. You need to calm down and stop being so irrational.

**Rebecca:**

Here we go again. I am not being paranoid or irrational. You always make me doubt my own memory and perceptions. Michael, you are trying to control me.

**Michael:**

You're being ridiculous. I'm done talking to you when you're like this.

**Rebecca:**

Now, you're done because I won't let you get away with it. Are we just gonna pretend that everything is ok?

*They both are caught up in their emotions and are in a fight. Michael might not be intending to gaslight Rebecca—he might be reacting defensively without any larger negative intent than to avoid blame. Someone knowingly gaslighting their partner can cause major psychological harm, but if Michael's doing it by accident they can step out of this negative cycle of interaction and things can turn around. So, let's go with this concept that he's doing it by accident: if Michael owns up to it, the conversation can totally go like this.*

**Michael:**

Rebecca, although I hate to admit it, I'm sorry. I was wrong here. I take full responsibility for my actions

*Taking accountability is a huge deal, especially for someone used to reacting defensively, as it requires putting the ego aside.*

**Rebecca:**

Thank you for acknowledging that, Michael. It means a lot to me.

*A little positive reinforcement can go a long way to help people improve their behaviour. But in a therapy session, counsellors would also encourage both clients to connect with the emotions that might coming up for Rebecca as she hears those words. Is she feeling heard and understood? Hopeful for the relationship? Is she skeptical and not sure if he can keep it up in the long term?*

**Michael:**

I know I have a lot of work to do to be a better partner. I will try not to walk away. I'm willing to do the work and make things right.

**Rebecca:**

Omg Michael. This is a first. I appreciate that, and I'm willing to work on this with you. We have to find healthy ways to communicate.

Our brain is experience-based and these positive interactions, associated emotions and the impact of these interactions on our thinking patterns can have a long-lasting impact on our relationships.

# CHAPTER 8

—

# Shoutout to My Baby

## Appreciation and gratitude for our partners

We are often so caught up in our day-to-day lives that we don't appreciate our partners. Do you thank your partner for the things they do for you? Do you tell them what they mean to you? It's so easy to take them for granted in the hectic rush of life, but that can create feelings of resentment.

Appreciating and expressing gratitude might be easy for some and not so much for others. When we show our partners that we value and appreciate them, it can make them feel good about themselves as long as it is genuine and done in a way that makes sense to them. Do they like acknowledgement through words or in a different way?

One way to show appreciation and gratitude towards your partner is through verbal affirmations. Take the time to tell your partner how much you appreciate them and all that they do for you. This can be as simple as thanking them for making dinner or expressing gratitude for their support during a difficult time.

Another way to show appreciation is through small acts of kindness and thoughtfulness. This could be something as simple as surprising your partner with their favourite coffee in the morning or leaving a thoughtful note for them to find. This could be through acts of service, such as taking on a task that your partner normally handles, or simply being there for them when they need support. These small gestures can go a long way in making your partner feel loved and appreciated.

When my private practice became busy, I needed my partner to pick up children from school, and he knew that I would adjust my schedule when he had to take work trips. He knows I like it when he brings me back dark chocolate from his expeditions and that is his way of showing appreciation for what I do for our children and for our marriage.

**Here's a couple who realized they were taking each other for granted:**

*Sonia and Jon have been together for a few years, but lately, Sonia has been feeling undervalued and unappreciated by Jon. If she examines her own behaviours carefully, she recognizes she has also been distant.*

*She wants to work on improving their relationship by developing her own appreciation skills and hoping Jon will also start becoming more present. For her, the journey was to muster up enough courage to bring these issues up and then assure herself that they can overcome these hurdles.*

### Sonia:

Hey Jon, something has been on my mind lately. Can we talk for a minute please? I've been feeling a little neglected lately. I'll admit I have been distant too. I want us to work on expressing more appreciation and gratitude towards you.

### Jon:

Wow Sonia. I had no clue you have been feeling this way. What's been going on?

### Sonia:

I feel like I don't tell you often enough how much I appreciate you and all that you do for me. I know I can be critical at times, and I want to work on being more positive and supportive. Sorry, I have been so distracted lately.

**Jon:**

I appreciate that, Sonia. I know I can be a little oblivious at times and I assume all is well if we are not fighting.

**Sonia:**

Great. So, one thing I'd like to start right away is noticing small things that you do for us on a regular basis. How hard would it be for you to show me the same level of appreciation? Can we set a goal to say something positive and appreciative to each other at least once a day?

*Now Jon can go either way.*

**Jon:**

Do we really have to do that? We want to do so many things and nothing gets done. Just another thing on my plate. Are you going to be critical if we forget to do it sometimes?

*Constructively planning for the next time, we get caught up in the storm of these emotions and beliefs is important, so Jon is raising an important point (though he could definitely do it in a more supportive way.) Another response could be*

**Jon:**

Absolutely. I think that's a great idea.

**Sonia:**

Great. I didn't think it would be so easy and you'll be so receptive. Let's start right away. I'll go first. Jon, I really appreciate how hard you work for us and how much you care about keeping our yard pretty.

*Notice she is being encouraging here.*

**Jon:**

Thank you, Sonia. That means a lot to me. I didn't think you cared about the yard. I thought you resented all the time I spent outside fixing things. I like how you always make sure that the fridge is stocked, and the toilet paper is readily available.

In this scenario, Sonia, and Jon both demonstrate an understanding of the value of expressing appreciation and gratitude in their relationship. They are able to have a positive and open conversation about their feelings, and they are able to set a goal to express appreciation towards each other on a daily basis. You can have relationship goals and can fall off the wagon but it's crucial to consistently show up and to keep trying especially when things are hard.

Developing new patterns isn't easy, and sometimes it is ok to fall back on common values, interests, and the initial attraction that we felt for our romantic partners.

Social psychology research indicates that the factors that keep people liking and loving each other in long-term relationships are at least in part the same as the factors that lead to initial attraction—so then why not appreciate the things you've always liked about them? The fact that your partner still keeps fit (making their self-care a priority is an asset for your relationship), or the sense of humour (could be a great way to diffuse some tension in the interactions), the passion (for their interests, their career, or home improvements) the cleverness or kindness that drew them to you in the first place. Notice when they take care of you or do something they know you like and let them know you noticed.

**Let's take a peek at another celebrity example.** I'll share what I see in Tom Hanks and Rita Wilson's relationship and what we, as seekers of strong relationships, can learn from it.

Tom has been one of my favourite actors since *Forrest Gump* and, like many other fans, I want to know more about him—and one of his favourite things to talk to the media about is his love story.

Rita and Tom met in the 80s and got married in 1988. They have faced many challenges and changes, including Tom Hanks' rise to fame and Rita Wilson's battle with breast cancer. However, they have always remained committed to each other and have shown others the importance of communication, appreciating each other, riding the wave together, compromise, and mutual respect in maintaining a strong and loving relationship.

In an interview with *People* magazine, Tom Hanks said, "Rita and I have a deep and abiding love for one another. We're very much in the same business, so we understand each other's lives and demands. We've been through a lot together and we know how to work through difficult times."

Wilson has also talked about the importance of regular conversations and supporting each other. She says, "We talk to each other. We respect each other. We support each other. We have a lot of fun together. And we're in it for the long haul."

How beautiful and inspiring! When we have so many options out there, it can be easy to get distracted and to jump ship when things become tough, or to catastrophize and think it's over. At the end of the day, we can either focus on what's tearing us apart or what's keeping us together—and hopefully it's much more than just "the children." We've got to appreciate the wonderful things about our partners to keep our relationships strong.

# CHAPTER 9

## Don't Mute Me

**Intimacy beyond heart emojis**

I wanted to touch on this topic as it comes up quite frequently in our couples' therapy work. Going back to the basics, let's look at Steinberg's model of love and relationships[7]. This model proposes that there are four stages of love: limerence, attraction, attachment, and consummate love.

1. **Limerence** is the initial stage of love, characterized by intense feelings of infatuation and attraction. This is often described as the "honeymoon phase" of a relationship, where everything feels new and exciting.

A couple who just started dating might be in the limerence stage, spending all their time together and feeling those butterflies in their stomachs.

Sometimes I tell my clients to take it slow and easy—all those raging love hormones can make you go too fast, too soon. It's important to take things at a reasonable pace, to protect yourself from hurt. It's important to upgrade slowly, continuously, and consistently to get the relationship to the place it needs to be for the happiness of the people involved.

7    Sternberg RJ. A triangular theory of love. *Psychol Rev.* 1986;93(2):119-135. doi:10.1037/0033-295x.93.2.119

2. **Attraction** is the second stage of love, characterized by strong feelings of affection and a deep connection with one's partner. At this stage, couples may begin to consider a long-term commitment, such as moving in together or getting married.

A couple who has been dating for a few years and is thinking about getting married might be in the attraction stage of love.

3. **Attachment** is the third stage of love, characterized by a sense of comfort and security with one's partner. At this stage, couples may feel more settled and at ease with each other and may prioritize maintaining a strong connection with their partner.

A couple who has been married for several years and has children together might be in the attachment stage of love.

4. **Consummate love** is the final stage of love, characterized by a deep and unconditional love for one's partner. At this stage, couples may feel a strong sense of commitment and a deep connection with each other.

A couple who has been together for several decades and has a strong bond might be in the consummate love stage. These are the couples I aspire to be like.

In order to maintain intimacy in long-term relationships, we have to prioritize communication, connection, and understanding. Once the communication is over, the relationship is done. This may involve regularly setting aside time for one-on-one conversations, finding ways to show affection and appreciation towards each other, and making an effort to understand and support each other's needs. It's building a memory book together. Folks who are open and vulnerable with each other can foster a deeper level of intimacy.

Did you see a deep level of intimacy between couples while growing up? Once the initial honeymoon phase is over, if enough effort isn't put in, the attraction and infatuation fade away. While the early parts of a relationship can be an exciting and enjoyable time, it's normal for that honeymoon phase to eventually come to an end. Don't let this scare you.

**Maintain warmth and rekindle the love in your relationship by:**

1. Doing an **assessment**. Take a step back and evaluate what's been working and what hasn't been working in your relationship. What were some of the things that made you feel connected and loved at

the beginning of your relationship? How can you bring those things back into your relationship?

2. Making an effort to **prioritize** your relationship. Set aside time for one-on-one conversations and activities and make an effort to show your partner appreciation and affection.

3. Tapping into **Novelty and Curiosity**. How is your person changing and transforming? Are they growing wiser or are you seeing a different side of them that you did not see earlier? Be curious about this new side. Have you considered trying new things together? Going on new adventures and trying novel experiences can help to inject some excitement back into your relationship.

4. Practising **good communication**. Could you say things differently or at a better time? What do you need to say that you are unable to express or what are they seeing that you are not getting?

Overall, rekindling love when the honeymoon phase is over requires effort and commitment from both partners. One person cannot do it all alone: there has to be a healthy buy-in from both sides. I have seen relationships transform completely when people make an effort to prioritize their relationship, communicate openly and honestly, and maintain their sense of awe.

## *Making Time*

It can be challenging to find time for each other when both partners are busy with work, family, and other commitments. Here are some proven ways, tried and tested by successful couples, you can use if you are struggling or are feeling disconnected:

**Schedule regular date nights.** Set aside a specific day and time each week for a date night. This can be a chance to have a special outing or activity together and reconnect without distractions. But it doesn't work if you're checked out—so mute your group chats and really become present in the moment to connect with your partner at a deeper level. You'd be surprised how many times I've heard couples complain that "my partner is in a relationship with their phone,"—one, or even both, members of a couple feeling replaced by video games and doom scrolling.

**Take advantage of small moments.** Look for opportunities to spend small amounts of time together throughout the day. For example, you could have breakfast together in the morning, go for a walk after dinner, or spend a few minutes talking before bed. When was the last time you checked out that cute coffee shop together near your home or work?

**Plan weekend getaways.** Consider taking a weekend trip or vacation together to spend quality time together and disconnect from daily responsibilities. Don't wait for things to go bad or you burn out before making this change. Add this in your routine if it is sustainable to have periodic getaway breaks where technology cannot touch you or demand your attention. Turn this attention towards your partner.

**Make time for hobbies and activities you both enjoy.** Do things together that you both enjoy, whether it's cooking, hiking, going to concerts, and music festivals, exercising, or spending time in nature.

No, my friends, watching Netflix together in silence is not engaging with each other—you're both focused on the TV instead of each other. You both are allowed to watch your favourite shows (hopefully one partner is not hogging the TV all the time and TV watching time is fairly distributed) but you get connection out of it when you can both turn towards each other and have meaningful conversations about what you liked or disliked about the shows you watched.

If you both enjoy gaming, evaluate—is it too much? Are you interacting with each other? Couch co-op might be a dying art form, but if you want to connect as a couple, it's crucial to actually be talking when you play games. Do you do other things together that aren't mediated by a game?

**Use technology to stay connected.** Technology is not all bad. If you can't be physically together, use technology to your advantage and stay connected. This can include video calls, phone calls, or even sending each other texts or emails throughout the day.

On a recent family trip, I was opposed to bringing the game consoles with us and wanted everyone to turn off their phones—but my children had downloaded party games we could all play together. They were human and interactive, and brought us closer together instead of leaving us disconnected.

Although I must admit, I missed playing Scattergories with the board all spread out on the table, in the end everyone was having a good time and we had quality family time—so that's a win in my book.

## *Boredom*

Sometimes, if intimacy isn't carefully maintained, a relationship can degrade over time. One of my clients (who had been married for a long time) once mentioned to me that she couldn't pinpoint what was wrong in her relationship. She said, *"Maybe I am bored of being married—or maybe I find my partner boring."* Have you ever felt that way about a partner?

My colleagues and I often discuss scenarios like this and offer theories about what could have created that distance. Perhaps she has been busy with her career and the bond between her, and her husband has become weak. In cases like that I wonder—was it strong in the first place?

There are lots of reasons people can lose their bond over time. Did the struggles of life pull them apart, or did they simply grow apart as their personalities changed? Did they meet other people in their lives who were more interesting to be intimate with?

Family life can also cause a bond to degrade. Was it that they gave everything to their children and had nothing left for each other? Once the children grew up and flew away, instead of their romance rekindling, did they turn their attention to easier sources of nurture and forget about each other? The bottom line is, there could be many different reasons for boredom.

**If you find that you are feeling bored in your relationship, I suggest starting by being open and honest about it with your partner.** We all deserve transparency, and our partners need to know our truth. They are not mind readers and can't fix what they're not aware is a problem.

As we discuss the issue with our partner, we can identify what needs to be done to repair the rupture of the bond. Discussing what our innermost desires are, what unmet attachment needs lie beneath surface-level issues, and where we are not feeling fulfilled can spark a conversation that leads to a profound shift in our relationship. If you've had these conversations and they have gone nowhere, however, then that's a whole other ball game. But if both partners are on board, there are a few things you can do to address boredom in a relationship.

**Identify the root cause.** It may be helpful to try to identify the underlying cause of your boredom. When did you start feeling disconnected from your partner? Are you not spending enough quality time together? Are you lacking shared interests or activities? Understanding the root cause of your boredom can help you and your partner address the issue and find ways to reconnect.

**Try new things.** Tap into curiosity and creativity. I am all about new dishes, new movies and new places and my partner likes to stick to tried and tested. He can watch his favourite movies again and again, while I seek novelty. His rationale about going to a restaurant where he is familiar with the food and dishes is that he won't be disappointed. We've come to a mutual understanding in terms of how much novelty, creativity, curiosity, and playfulness we bring into our lives.

Doing new things together can help to break up the routine and add excitement to the relationship. This could be something as simple as trying a new hiking trail, going on a day trip, or something more adventurous like trying a new hobby or activity together at least once. Novelty can add spice back into your lacklustre relationship—as long as the foundation is strong, and there is a sense of safety in it for both partners.

**Explore each other's interests.** Spending time doing activities that your partner enjoys can help to deepen your understanding with them and you get to be part of a piece of their world.

I once hyped up a hot yoga class for my partner, and he came to one with me and almost died of heat. Needless to say, he did not become a member at my favourite yoga studio—but he will indulge my desires from time to time to keep me happy. And yes, I have tried sitting and watching NBA games with him, and even tried my hand at a basketball game or two, though I am no athlete and will probably fail miserably if quizzed about players or teams. Nonetheless, we have found a list of things over the past 19 years that we both enjoy. I tell my clients that by exploring each other's interests you are sending a message to your partner, telling them that they are a priority and you do care for them and what they like.

**Get inspired by having conversations with others.** If you are struggling to find ways to reconnect with your partner or are feeling overwhelmed by the ideas, it may be helpful to seek guidance from your friends or family members who are in successful relationships. They might be able to provide solutions and guidance that you need. You can also always talk to a therapist—and no, things don't need to be bad to get some help from a trusted professional.

Where there is a will, there is a way. You can certainly find ways to improve your relationship but start small and take one step at a time. Too much, too soon, too fast can be like driving in a fast lane but with a car not equipped for the wild ride.

**Here are a few ideas you can try, whether you're struggling with boredom or just enjoying keeping the fire lit:**

- Go on a road trip or take a vacation to a new destination. This can be a great opportunity to explore a new place and create new memories together.
- Try a new outdoor activity, such as hiking, rock climbing, or kayaking. Perhaps some camping—or glamping—or an exotic new thing (at least for me, anyway) like mud baths. This can be a great way to bond and let your inner child out.
- Attend a live event or performance, such as a concert, theatre production, or sporting event. This can be a fun and exciting way to spend an evening together.
- Learn something new together—take a painting or pottery class. This can be a relaxing and creative way to spend time together.
- Take a tour to a winery or brewery. This can be a fun and educational way to learn about different types of wine or beer if that interests you.
- Chase some thrills together. On my personal bucket list has been the idea of going on a hot air balloon ride or taking a helicopter tour. I am a thrill seeker—but I am not sure if my husband would enjoy that idea.
- Sweat together! Try a new exercise class such as yoga, pilates, or boxing. This can be a great way to stay active and see if you find each other attractive after a sweaty workout.
- Eat something new—foodies can go on a food tour, or try a new type of cuisine.
- Make up your own traditions and rituals as a couple, around holidays or other significant days.

Do remember that all relationships have ups and downs, and it is normal to experience periods of boredom or disconnection. The big question is if you can reconnect successfully, or if you feel you are constantly hitting a brick wall. Trust your own ability to communicate openly and honestly with your partner. Seek support when it's needed and work together to address any challenges you think your relationship is facing.

Don't let boredom suck the life out of your emotional connection. Don't let your conversation dwindle down to text messages or sharing memes. Hold hands, go for a walk, and talk about what truly matters to you.

# Chapter 10

# Boosting Engagement

## Coping with hard times as a couple

When the stressors of life—like careers and bill payments, the health of our family members, parenting, or education—build up and sap our energy, expressing our love and affection can take a back seat. We might even start becoming short with our person or snap. We might seek other distractions to cope with life, forgetting that expressing our love and affection can actually be comforting and soothing when reciprocated.

**Science suggests some of these ways to maintain our love during difficult times:**
- **Verbal affirmations.** Take the time to tell your partner how much you love and appreciate them. This could be as simple as saying "I love you" or expressing gratitude for specific things your partner does for you.
- **Physical affection.** Show your love and affection through physical touch, and it could be as simple as hugging, kissing, holding hands, cuddling, or engaging in sex.

- **Acts of kindness and thoughtfulness.** Try small gestures like making your partner's favourite meal or leaving a thoughtful note for them to find.
- **Quality time.** Make an effort to set aside time for one-on-one activities with your partner. This could be anything from going on a special date to simply sitting down and having a deep conversation where you can pour your heart out.

Expressing and nurturing love and affection in a relationship requires effort and commitment from both partners—and if one is exhausted or going through some personal stuff, it can be very hard to go into that that state of social engagement and feeling open to experiences (that ventral vagal state we discussed earlier). Don't put your relationship on the back burner when everything in life is demanding more attention. By making an effort to show love and affection towards your partner, you are sending a message that they're worth the time. You might be surprised at how much it helps you, too!

**Here's a couple who works through disconnection when times get tough:**

*Sara and Mike have been together for a few years, but lately, they've been feeling a little disconnected as Sara is burning out from the exhaustion of her teaching job, struggling with the loss of her father, and estranged from her mother.*

*Mike decides to be more present for the children so Sara can have some "me time"—even though he's in the process of setting up his new business. They want to have regular date nights where they can focus on each other and have deep conversations, but time and money are constraints.*

*They can start small by saying "I love you" more often and doing small acts of kindness, like making each other's favourite meals or running errands for each other. Perhaps they simply need to let go of some commitments temporarily, while they're navigating stressful times. They reach out for help from friends and extended family members and create space with each other to explore their feelings.*

**And here's another couple who keeps the appreciation coming:**

*Joe and Jessica are working towards accepting each other's families and also making an effort to support each other's goals and dreams.*

*Jessica takes on more household responsibilities to allow Joe to focus on his master's degree, and Joe encourages Jessica to pursue her passion for painting by setting up a studio space for her. It might take time, but consistent efforts to strengthen our bonds with the ones we love can pay off.*

**I also admire the love and affection of Oprah Winfrey and Stedman Graham.** Oprah and Stedman have been together for over three decades, and they have a marvellous relationship.

One thing that has contributed to the success of their relationship is their ability to prioritize their individual goals and passions. Oprah has had a successful career as a media mogul and philanthropist, and Stedman has had a successful career as an author and businessman. Despite their busy schedules, they have always made time for each other and have supported each other's pursuits.

Another thing that has contributed to the success of their relationship is their strong communication skills. Oprah and Stedman are open and honest with each other about their feelings and needs, and they make an effort to listen and understand each other. Their relationship helps us see the value of individual growth, strong communication, and mutual support in any relationship.

### *Communication and Individual Growth*

I know of many successful and happily married couples in my circle of friends. When I have dinner table conversations with them, they will sometimes joke about it or say they are winging it, but honestly, in some long-lasting relationships, I have seen good communication, mutual respect, and a whole lot of understanding, emotional intelligence and commitment to each other.

One friend once said that they "never go to bed angry."

This can work for some, but sometimes we have to carefully choose time for tough conversations—and right before bed when we are exhausted is not it. Nor is right before an important deadline when your partner is under a different level of stress and not really emotionally available.

I have also seen that in many quality relationships, folks prioritize their individual growth and independence within the relationship. They're committed to their success as a couple and happy to compromise, but they also maintain their own interests and ambitions. A healthy couple will encourage each other to pursue their passions and goals, and they make an effort to support each other's growth and development. They are each other's biggest cheerleaders, not each other's biggest competitors.

### Respect in Conflict

Respect is another component that we have to continuously re-introduce into our relationships. It can easily disintegrate after we know the not-so-cool parts of our partner—familiarity can easily breed contempt.

Traits like dishonesty, lack of effort, infidelity, neglecting responsibilities can all lead up to this "sitcom marriage". It shouldn't be surprising, even after twenty years or forty years or sixty years of marriage, for someone to like and enjoy their partner.

Belittling, criticizing, and dead-end arguing can all be detrimental for relationships. The re-introduction of respect might start with really listening to what they have to say and engaging with them in a meaningful conversation. It's important to be considerate, and to honour other person's boundaries and preferences. Allowing ourselves to evolve and grow within the relationship—recognizing when we need to do something more or differently—is hard. It's too easy to get defensive when you feel criticized but try to respect what your partner needs.

### Forgiveness

People mess up. Sometimes, our partners are going to hurt us, and we have to make a choice to forgive them or see the relationship end. It is totally a personal choice, and everyone's process for it is different. Forgiveness is not always easy, and it may take time and effort to fully forgive someone.

Forgiveness allows individuals to move past mistakes and conflicts and rebuild trust and connection with their partners. If you're having trouble forgiving your partner, it's important to communicate your needs and boundaries. Let your partner know how their actions have impacted you and what you need in order to move forward.

If you've been betrayed in some capacity, it's important to acknowledge and validate your own feelings before attempting to forgive your partner. Take the time to process your emotions and allow yourself to feel whatever you're feeling.

People who have been betrayed have asked me a lot of difficult questions in the clinic. What if they forgive their partner and their partner does it again? How do they even get past the insecurities that came from the betrayal to start the process? How do they forgive and start to trust? Should they forgive their partner at all? There are so many variables that can affect the situation. The extent of hurt someone experiences is unique to each person and the context.

One woman told me that it wasn't the fact that he betrayed her trust that hurt the most, but the fact that he lied about it. His explanation was that he was afraid to lose her, so he panicked and lied. Once caught red handed, he was embarrassed and ashamed but got angry every time she brought the subject up.

She wanted some sort of relief from her emotional pain. He wondered if she would ever truly forgive him for a mistake, he had made under peer pressure. They were caught up in this vicious cycle of thoughts with no end in sight.

Practising forgiveness can often be difficult, especially if we have been deeply hurt or betrayed by someone we care about so much. When we are loyal, we need loyalty in return. When we are kind, we want kindness.

**If you're struggling to forgive someone, even when you want to, try following these steps:**

1. **Acknowledge your feelings.** Allow yourself to feel and express any hurt, anger, or pain that you may be experiencing. This can help you process your emotions and begin to move past them.

2. **Take time to reflect**. Consider the circumstances surrounding the event that caused you pain. Was the person acting out of character, or were they struggling with their own issues? What triggered the situation? Understanding the context of what happened can help you to see things from their perspective and be more open to forgiveness.

3. **Communicate with the person.** Talk to the person who has hurt you and express how their actions made you feel. It can be helpful to approach this conversation with an open and non-judgmental mindset, and to focus on finding a resolution rather than placing blame.

4. **Practice self-care.** Forgiveness isn't easy, so you must take care of yourself during this time. Engage in activities that bring you joy and help you to relax and seek support from friends or a therapist if needed.

5. **Make a decision.** Decide whether or not you are ready to forgive the person who has hurt you. This is a personal decision that only you can make, and it is important to do what feels right for you.

Remember that forgiveness is not about forgetting what happened or denying the pain you felt. It is about letting go of negative emotions and moving forward with a sense of understanding and compassion. By practising forgiveness, you can be a bigger person and create a stronger, more positive relationship with the people you care about.

**Here's a couple I worked with who chose forgiveness, and who and rebuilt their relationship when it was crumbling:**

*Jasmine and Patrick had been together for five years, and things had always been pretty good between them. However, over the past year, they had been going through a rough patch. They were both working long hours and had very little time for each other, and they had been arguing a lot.*

*One day, while they were out shopping, Patrick received a text message from an old flame. Jasmine saw the message and became extremely upset, feeling hurt and betrayed by Patrick's lack of loyalty. She accused him of cheating and demanded to know why he was still in contact with his ex.*

*Patrick, feeling guilty and ashamed, admitted that he had been struggling with feelings for his ex and had been trying to figure out how to deal with them. He apologized profusely and begged for Jasmine's forgiveness.*

*Jasmine was heartbroken and hurt, but after some reflection, she realized that she loved Patrick and wanted to work through their problems together. She decided to forgive him and to try to move past this incident.*

*Over the next few weeks, Jasmine and Patrick made an effort to spend more quality time together, setting some parameters around how to deal with the situation if it arose again and how to be more transparent with each other. Couples' therapy worked for them, and they were able to rebuild their relationship and move forward in a positive and loving way.*

*In the end, Jasmine's decision to forgive Patrick saved their relationship and allowed them to move past their problems and create a stronger, more fulfilling bond.*

# CHAPTER 11

## #RelationshipGoals

### Shared goals and outside influences

Last but not least, I want to touch on the idea of having shared goals and values. When two people share similar goals and values, they are able to align their priorities and work towards some common objectives, which can bring them closer together and strengthen their bond. Shared goals could be anything—having the financial freedom to travel or to buy a house, raising children together, building a business together or championing a political cause.

Having shared goals and values can also provide a sense of purpose and direction in a relationship, which can help to keep the passion alive. When two people are working towards something that is important to both of them, it can be a source of inspiration and motivation for both partners.

In the past, my partner and I used digital platforms to work on some common projects and shared ideas. We've discovered new activities, new restaurants to try out and causes to care about thanks to technology. When we were engaged and doing long distance, yahoo messenger was our saviour. Our shared goal was for me to come to Canada.

Nowadays, I have seen that if we are not careful with our time, we can end up spending too much of it on social media. Digital distractions can easily take away from the time that couples could be spending together or using to work towards their shared goals. It can also create a sense of competition or inadequacy, with couples feeling the pressure to keep up with the lifestyles that they see online. But don't forget that the couples you see on Instagram are only showing you their best side—people rarely post fights, exhaustion, and dirty dishes on their profiles.

In the digital age, we're exposed to more half-baked opinions than ever before, and on some very important issues the facts can be hard to pin down. Digital media can expose couples to conflicting or opposing viewpoints, which can lead to disagreements or misunderstandings. This can be particularly challenging if couples have different values or beliefs, as the extremes of opinion and questionable sources online can amplify these differences and create tension in the relationship.

I have worked with a couple where one partner, to support their viewpoint, would find articles, videos or social media posts promoting his perspective. While it's generally a good idea to support your viewpoints and couples can have very productive discussions from different starting points, he was using them as a "gotcha". This was disturbing for his partner. We can find all kind of awful information online, too—and by that, I mean extremist viewpoints or information from unreliable sources.

Having honest conversations can help couples align their goals. Many times, collaboration, compromise and flexibility are required to be open to new challenges, whether they're minor home renovations or the decision to move across the country.

### *External Influences*

These vital decisions—as well as the overall health of a partnership—can be influenced by external forces. I worked with a couple who moved from India to escape family drama but then one partner had to go back to resolve some legal matters, leaving the wife alone with the toddler. Years later, when they connected with me, the wife still held bitterness about the time when she needed her partner, and he wasn't there. In any adult romantic relationship, there are various external forces that can have an impact on the dynamic between the two partners. These external forces can range from work and family obligations to societal expectations and cultural norms.

One common external force that can influence adult romantic relationships is work. When one or both partners have demanding careers, it can be difficult to find time for each other and to maintain a healthy balance between work and personal life. This can lead to feelings of resentment and frustration as both partners feel like they're being neglected, and if children are in the picture, it becomes even more complicated.

Societal expectations and cultural norms can also play a role in influencing adult romantic relationships. For example, certain cultures may place a greater emphasis on traditional gender roles and family dynamics, which can impact how a couple relates to each other and to the outside world. In couples with different backgrounds, this can cause a lot of internal friction.

Another external force that can influence adult romantic relationships is family. When one or both partners come from different family backgrounds or have conflicting values and expectations, it can be challenging to find a way to integrate these differences into the relationship. This can lead to conflicts and misunderstandings that can strain the relationship.

External forces such as these can create challenges and barriers for couples, but they can also provide opportunities for growth and understanding. By being aware of these external forces and learning how to navigate them together, couples can build a stronger and more resilient relationship.

### Extended Families

While families can have a significant influence on our romantic relationships, both positive and negative, it is vital to have some boundaries and expectations around the roles of extended family in a couple's life. Support and guidance from our families can help to strengthen our relationships—for example, if we have grown up in a family with strong communication skills and healthy conflict-resolution techniques, we may be more likely to use these skills in our romantic relationships.

My maternal grandmother passed away when my mother was eight years old and my grandfather never remarried. My grandfather's job was moving around, so sometimes my mother spent time with her older brother, sister, or extended family members. She didn't have a very good model for constancy in her father, so she struggled to work things out when they went wrong.

When my parents' relationship was undergoing a rough period and my mother wanted to separate and divorce my dad, my paternal grandparents stepped in and guided them to a more stable place that sort of worked out for them. In this way, my grandparents helped my parents resolve some of their issues.

Our families can also have negative influences on our romantic relationships. In much of my trauma work (especially intergenerational), I have witnessed firsthand that if someone has grown up in a family with unhealthy communication patterns, family secrets, or unresolved conflicts, they tend to repeat these patterns in their romantic relationships.

Additionally, if our families have different values or expectations, it can be challenging to integrate these differences into our romantic relationships. For example, if one partner comes from a family that places a high value on traditional gender roles, while the other partner comes from a family that is more progressive in their views, it can be difficult to find a balance that makes everyone comfortable. To address the influence of families on our romantic relationships, the first step is to be aware as to how our families may be impacting our behaviours and to have those difficult conversations as a couple, and then to do something about it.

**Here's a couple who found themselves caught between two very different sets of expectations:**

*Laura and Alex had been together for seven years and were very much in love. They had their ups and downs, but they were excited to take the next step in their relationship by getting married.*

*However, as they began to plan their wedding, they started to notice that their extended families were causing some tension in their relationship. Laura's parents were very traditional and had high expectations for the wedding, while Alex's parents were more laid back and didn't seem to care as much about the details.*

*As the planning process continued, the tension between the two families only seemed to grow. Laura's parents were constantly criticizing Alex's family's ideas and decisions, while Alex's parents were feeling left out and uninvolved.*

*Despite their best efforts to keep the peace, Laura and Alex found themselves caught in the middle of a battle between their two families. They were so focused on trying to make everyone happy that they didn't even realize how much the tension was impacting their own relationship.*

*Eventually, things came to a head and Laura and Alex had a big argument about the wedding. They were both struggling and overwhelmed by the pressure from their families that they couldn't even see how their own relationship was suffering. They thought they were stressed about the wedding, but it was not until they sat down and had a heart-to-heart conversation that they realized how much the influence of their extended families had been negatively impacting their relationship. They thought it was selfish to put their needs first but also realized that it was impossible to please everyone. So even though siblings and in-laws had their own Pinterest boards for how things should be, Laura and Alex decided to do things their own way.*

### Enmeshed Boundaries

Enmeshed boundaries occur when family members are overly involved in each other's lives, resulting in a lack of autonomy and individuality. When individuals grow up with enmeshed boundaries, it can be a struggle later on in their lives. It can appear as if they are simply very close to their family, but sometimes that's not the case. This type of boundary pattern can have a significant impact on adult romantic relationships, as individuals may struggle to establish healthy boundaries with their partners or may struggle to maintain a sense of identity separate from their family.

One potential impact of enmeshed boundaries is difficulty in establishing emotional intimacy in romantic relationships. Individuals who have grown up with enmeshed boundaries may have difficulty expressing their emotions, setting personal boundaries, or recognizing their own needs and desires. Other struggles can include difficulty with conflicts. They may have a problem asserting themselves, expressing their opinions, or compromising with their partners, which can lead to ongoing conflicts or feelings of resentment and dissatisfaction.

If you feel you have enmeshed boundaries, it can be helpful to develop more healthy and adaptive ways of interacting with others. Specifically, cognitive-behavioural therapy and emotion-focused therapy can be useful. These types of therapy can help individuals identify and challenge maladaptive patterns of thinking and behaviour and help them develop new coping strategies for dealing with challenging situations.

I encourage everyone to work on developing greater emotional regulation skills, assertiveness, and communication skills, so that healthy boundaries can be maintained in our romantic relationships. Active listening, empathy, and conflict-resolution strategies can help couples deal with difficult external forces and bring loving couples to a new level of emotional intimacy.

# Conclusion

To conclude, loneliness, feeling detached and disconnected in our relationships can lead to various mental health problems. We all deserve happy, healthy, and improved relationships. Over time, our emotional bonds should become strong and not deteriorate. If we can connect to the true essence of being human, which is to feel, then we can emotionally attune to our partners again and again, ultimately taking our love affair to the next level. The die-hard romantic in me wants to encourage readers to continue learning and growing in their adult romantic relationships. If you've lost the spark, there is definitely a way to rekindle it. Take our roadmap and give it a try.

A lot of things go into having a great relationship, so examine the ingredients and pick something to work on. Effective communication, setting and respecting boundaries, building and maintaining trust, managing and resolving conflict, maintaining and deepening intimacy, expressing and nurturing love and affection, showing and receiving respect, practising forgiveness, providing and seeking emotional support, and aligning goals and values and working towards shared objectives can all help you move towards stronger relationships, and working on any of them is likely to send ripples of improvement through your relationship.

It is possible to upgrade adult relationships with effort, communication, and a willingness to learn and grow together. All the aspects we've discussed in the book are interconnected and form the foundation for a strong and lasting partnership.

Readers, I hope you'll agree that technology can play a significant role in relationships, both positively and negatively. As we've seen, technology can enhance communication by providing channels for staying connected, such as texts, video calls, and social media platforms. It can bridge geographical distances and allow partners to express love, affection, and support in creative ways. Technology can also offer resources like relationship apps, online therapy, and educational materials to help couples strengthen their bond and address challenges.

However, like everything else, too much of something can cause imbalance in our lives.

In my clinical work, I have consistently seen that technology can exacerbate existing issues—an overly attached person can now spam-text their partner at work, someone with a wandering eye can easily find their next indiscretion on a dating site, doomscrolling can cause a partner prone to anxiety to panic even more when they do not get immediate reassurance from their partner, and much more. Research has also demonstrated strong associations between addictive use of technology and comorbid psychiatric disorders[8].

Technology can present various challenges. It can hinder effective communication if partners rely too heavily on digital interactions, leading to misinterpretation of messages or a lack of nonverbal cues. Technology can create distractions and take away quality time spent together, affecting intimacy and emotional connection. It may also contribute to breaches of trust, such as privacy invasions or online infidelity. Couples need to be mindful of their technology usage, set boundaries around its presence in their relationship, and ensure that face-to-face interactions and genuine connection are prioritized.

To navigate the impact of technology on relationships successfully, open, and honest communication is crucial. My hope is that if you are in a relationship, you'll discuss your technology preferences, establish boundaries, and find a balance that works for both partners.

---

8    Andreassen, C. S., Billieux, J., Griffiths, M. D., Kuss, D. J., Demetrovics, Z., Mazzoni, E., & Pallesen, S. (2016). The relationship between addictive use of social media and video games and symptoms of psychiatric disorders: A large-scale cross-sectional study. *Psychology of Addictive Behaviors, 30*(2), 252–262. https://doi.org/10.1037/adb0000160

Be open to trust-building activities like open access to each other's digital devices, when appropriate, and transparent conversations about online interactions. When working through your conflicts, add in humanness to the mix. Allow your conflict-resolution strategies to address technology-related issues and explore compromises. It's important to cultivate emotional support offline and create opportunities for quality time without technological distractions. By aligning goals and values, you can make intentional choices about technology use that strengthen your connection and takes it to the next level rather than diminish it.

Welcome to this new era of your true relationship upgrade.

# About the Author

ADITI JASRA (formally Sharma) was born in India and now lives in Coquitlam, BC, Canada with her family (husband, 3 children: a pre-teen, a teenager and a fur-baby) and has travelled the world to observe interactions between human beings. She is a Canadian certified (CCC), registered clinical counsellor (RCC), with a Master's in Counselling Psychology with several  additional certifications including training in the EFT model of couples therapy. She also has a strong foundation in the theories and techniques that are most effective in supporting couples and relationships from a trauma informed, culturally sensitive perspective.

At her practice, Wellness North Counselling in Metro Vancouver, BC, Canada, Aditi and her colleagues work with individuals, couples and families to address a wide range of issues, examining relationships from an attachment lens while applying different models ranging from family systems, Gottman to EFT to achieve positive therapeutic outcomes for folx they support. These approaches allow her and her team to get a deeper understanding of the underlying dynamics at play in their work. Using psychological principles and evidence based models, specific treatment plans are developed that meet the needs and goals of her community and clients. She is continuously working on improving her own relationships with friends and family and upgrading them to a better version.

www.wellnessnorth.ca/aditi-jasra